A DIFFERENT KIND OF POLITICS

READINGS ON THE ROLE OF HIGHER EDUCATION IN DEMOCRACY

Edited by Derek W. M. Barker and David W. Brown

Kettering Foundation Press

A Different Kind of Politics: Readings on the Role of Higher Education in Democracy is published by Kettering Foundation Press. The interpretations and conclusions contained in this book represent the views of the authors. They do not necessarily reflect the views of the Charles F. Kettering Foundation, its directors, or its officers.

For information about permission to reproduce selections from this book, write to:
    Permissions
    Kettering Foundation Press
    200 Commons Road
    Dayton, Ohio 45459

This book is printed on acid-free paper.

First edition, 2009

Manufactured in the United States of America
    ISBN: 978-0-923993-28-3
Library of Congress Control Number: 2009921434

CONTENTS

PREFACE

IN THE LAST FEW YEARS, the Kettering Foundation and its network of researchers have produced a large body of work on higher education and its democratic role. This volume brings these works together into a single publication to ask how the multiple lines of research reflect a coherent approach to democratic politics. What is the common thread that unites Kettering's research in higher education?

The struggle to reclaim the democratic mission of higher education institutions is part of a broader dynamic in contemporary politics, the deceptively simple problem that citizens feel shut out of politics. Lacking control over the problems that confront them, citizens feel frustrated and disconnected from the institutions that have power over their lives. One way to understand this problem is as an imbalance between the organic and the institutional components of democracy (others have described this same imbalance in terms of citizen-centered versus professional politics, or civic agency against technocracy).[1] In institutional approaches to politics, experts assume that complex political problems are largely administrative in nature and name them in technical terms that only they can act upon. Rather than empowering communities to act on their own, institutional approaches treat communities as dependent clients or passive recipients of help from above. Instead of building upon the knowledge of citizens, institutional politics sees experts as the exclusive producers of knowledge, which they disseminate to society. Most important, institutional politics sees experts and professional organizations rather than citizens as the primary actors in solving public problems.

---

[1]Harry Boyte, "Against the Current: Developing the Civic Agency of College Students," *Change* (May-June 2008); Cynthia M. Gibson, "Citizens at the Center: A New Approach to Civic Engagement" (Case Foundation, 2006).

In organic politics, citizens are the primary actors. Citizens are able to understand the problems that they confront and take meaningful action to address them. Although sporadic and individual acts of volunteerism and casual interactions to build social trust may be important supplements to organic politics, they are no substitute for collective action. Professionals can play an important role in organic politics, not as technocrats that solve problems *for* citizens, but rather as civic professionals working *with* citizens in a way that builds upon the knowledge, skills, and power that they bring to democracy. This type of politics can be observed in deliberative forums in which citizens come together to make decisions on public problems, self-organizing social and political networks that are strengthening local communities, and movements to reclaim the civic roots of various professions.

Unfortunately, politics as usual (not to be confused with politics broadly understood) assumes that democracy is exclusively a matter of institutional politics. As Randa Slim notes, the movement for global democracy has become equated with institutional designs, oppositional electoral politics, and technical assistance, rather than habits of citizenship, building civic capacities, and culture change.[2] Various government and civil society institutions are undergoing a crisis in legitimacy stemming from a lack of connection to organic politics. For example, instead of achieving legitimacy through practices of self-rule that citizens could "own" themselves, in the movement for greater "accountability" we are seeing largely futile attempts to create legitimacy through technical metrics developed and interpreted by experts. Institutions that are charged with important public functions (like the media and philanthropy) often speak of "civic engagement," but in practice they mean providing services to a needy and passive public or garnering public support for their own preconceived goals. Citizens are reduced to voting and otherwise acting as spectators on the outside of a system that remains obscure and over which they have no power.

With its important social role in educating future generations of citizens and producing cutting-edge knowledge to advance solutions to public problems, higher education is an obvious intervention point for making

---

[2]Randa Slim, "Facing the Challenges of Emerging Democracies," *Kettering Review* vol. 25, no. 1 (2007).

democracy work as it should. As Claire Snyder argues, until the development of the modern research university, education for citizenship was considered *the* mission of colleges and universities in the United States. Congregational colleges, people's colleges, historically black colleges, and the land-grant university movement all saw teaching, research, and service in broadly political terms.[3] This political understanding of education extends back to antiquity and the Greek concept of *paideia*.[4] In contemporary society, higher education also contains exciting examples of organic politics in this tradition, in which young people are learning to act as citizens, and professionals are engaging in self-critique leading to new practices in which citizens are treated as primary political actors. At the same time, however, higher education contains many of the worst examples of technocratic politics, with experts naming problems in technical terms and treating citizens as dependent clients even when intending to serve their interests. As a recent report by Public Agenda shows, civic engagement is simply not high on the agenda of institutional leaders or constituencies in the general public.[5] Does higher education exacerbate the politics of expertise and further shut citizens out of politics? Or will it return to its democratic mission?

To answer these questions, we have compiled a series of readings, along with reflective interviews conducted by David Brown, on the common themes of the research and its implications for citizen self-rule. The material is drawn primarily from the following recent publications:[6]

- *Speaking of Politics,* by Katy J. Harriger and Jill J. McMillan (Kettering Foundation Press, 2007), a monograph on a sustained institutional commitment to infusing education for democratic citizenship throughout a college curriculum and cocurriculum;

---

[3]R. Claire Snyder, "Should Higher Education Have a Civic Mission? Historical Reflections," in *Agent of Democracy: Higher Education and the HEX Journey*, ed. David Brown and Deborah Witte (Dayton, OH: Kettering Foundation Press, 2008), 53-75.

[4]Werner Jaeger, *Paideia: The Ideals of Greek Culture*, 3 vols. (New York: Oxford University Press, 1971).

[5]"I'm Just Not That into Politics: Public and Leadership Views on Higher Education and Civic Engagement" (New York, NY: Public Agenda, 2007).

[6]Excepts of previously published material are used with the permission of the authors. To improve readability, some sections have been edited without the use of ellipses and recapitalization at the authors' request.

- *Millennials Talk Politics*, by Abby Kiesa, Alexander P. Orlowski, Peter Levine, Deborah Both, Emily Hoban Kirby, Mark Hugo Lopez, and Karlo Barrios Marcelo (Center for Information & Research on Civic Learning & Engagement [CIRCLE] in collaboration with the Kettering Foundation, 2007), on the political attitudes of college students;
- *Voices of Hope* (Kettering Foundation Press, 2007), by Nan Kari and Nan Skelton, the story of the Jane Addams School, a "school for citizenship" that receives support from the Center for Democracy and Citizenship of the University of Minnesota;
- *Deliberation & the Work of Higher Education* (Kettering Foundation Press, 2008), edited by John Dedrick, Laura Grattan, and Harris Dientsfrey, a collection of innovative experiments using deliberation in the civic education of college students;
- *Higher Education Exchange* (*HEX*), a journal edited by David W. Brown and Deborah Witte, featuring essays and interviews on the roles of higher education institutions and academic professionals in democracy;
- *Agent of Democracy: Higher Education and the HEX Journey* (Kettering Foundation Press, 2008), edited by David W. Brown and Deborah Witte, a series of reflective essays on more than a decade of *HEX* research.

Chapter One is an introductory essay by Elizabeth Hollander and Matthew Hartley. They provide an overview of recent Kettering research and its role in responding to apolitical approaches to civic engagement.

Chapter Two brings together a series of projects related to the civic education of college students. According to the *Millennials Talk Politics* report by Abby Kiesa and colleagues, despite a sense of frustration with politics as usual, young people are interested in opportunities for meaningful political participation. Studies by David Cooper and Katy Harriger and Jill McMillan, together with a student perspective presented by Allison Crawford, suggest that deliberation offers young people an experience in a different kind of politics, in which they are treated as having a strong sense of civic agency.

Chapter Three explores the role of scholarship in democracy. Knowledge is increasingly central in the global economy, but also ever more specialized and technical in nature, and ever more obscure and inaccessible to citizens. Unfortunately, the dominant approaches to the production and communication of knowledge in academia are built on theories that emphasize detachment from society, and the reward structures in academia favor these traditional models of expertise. In recent years, new forms of scholarship have emerged that work cooperatively with citizens, simultaneously strengthening democracy and ensuring that scholarly work has greater social relevance. Beginning with Jay Rosen's 1997 essay, the turn toward public forms of scholarship has been a theme for over a decade in the *Higher Education Exchange*. The pieces by Harry Boyte and Scott Peters reflect on this work in light of recent developments in the conflict between technocracy and civic agency.

Chapter Four examines the relationship between higher education institutions and community-based organizations. Higher education institutions sometimes treat communities as spaces for civic agency, but more often they see external stakeholders as needy clients dependent upon expertise for technical assistance. Sean Creighton shows that these efforts look much more like politics as usual when seen from the perspective of the community partners. However, Nan Kari's and Nan Skelton's *Voices of Hope* and David Pelletier's profile tell stories of new institutional structures that contribute to communities' civic capacities and redefine the role of expertise.

Chapter Five addresses the question of who will lead the next generation of civic engagement efforts in higher education. Those who have the strongest sense of civic identity and experience the most intense frustration with their institutions appear to be mostly faculty. The pieces by Bill Doherty and Adam Weinberg give personal accounts of the deepest passions behind faculty engaged in civic work. If higher education is to align itself with democratic politics, the transformation is likely to begin with stories like these.

Finally, David Mathews concludes the book with his reflections on the continuing challenges to reconnecting higher education to organic democracy. Although Mathews sees the work compiled in this volume as part of a growing democratic shift within higher education, he also sees this movement as critically limited. As he argues, the next generation of civic work in higher education will require building new relationships with external practitioners and stakeholders so that the civic engagement of higher education institutions will be relevant to the most urgent needs of communities.

The picture of higher education that emerges is thus highly ambivalent. Politics as usual appears to be the dominant trend within higher education, with a lack of attention to the civic dimensions of undergraduate education, detachment and obscurity in academic scholarship, and dysfunctional relationships between higher education institutions and communities. At the same time, there appears to be a growing sense of crisis within higher education, as well as innovative experiments at the margins to redefine teaching, research, and service. These efforts reflect a different kind of politics, with pedagogies that treat students as active learners and engaged citizens, new forms of professionalism that understand citizens as the primary actors in politics, and institutional efforts to build genuinely democratic relationships with community partners. This narrative, deeply critical of politics as usual, but cautiously optimistic about a different kind of politics, is not, of course, unique to higher education. Civic engagement efforts in higher education reflect a much larger global contest over the meaning of democracy, between democracy defined as the way of life of active citizens engaged in self-rule and democracy defined as an institutional arrangement with citizens playing a secondary role.

Derek Barker
Kettering Foundation

Introductory Essay: Reimagining the Civic Imperative of Higher Education

IMAGINE A UNIVERSITY that has deliberately and persistently built meaningful relationships with members of its wider community—neighborhood groups, community-based organizations, local citizens, nonprofits, and governmental agencies. Imagine that at this university, in their first-year, students begin to see how a variety of disciplinary lenses can be employed to understand important issues facing their institution, the local area, and larger society. In subsequent years of study, students come to understand the various policy levers by which participatory democratic change can be enacted—on campus and off. Students would learn the precepts of democratic deliberation and be invited to witness and later participate in various forums in which local, national, and global issues are debated and discussed. Soon, many students at this institution know more about the democratic processes of the local area than they would about their own hometowns. Further, community concerns that emerge from various deliberative forums would inform the development of service-learning projects and the service-learning experiences would lead to further debate and discussion about how to make additional progress. Research groups that draw on the expertise of various disciplines and of community members who are well versed in the local context would collaborate to develop a richer understanding of the issues and what might be done to improve the situation. The institution also would support research on the impact of various efforts.

This is the rich, formative educational experience that can be envisioned if the perspectives and practices articulated in the body of works published by the Kettering Foundation (and reviewed here) are integrated into college and university efforts to educate students for active citizenship. In doing so, the civic engagement movement in higher education might find an antidote to its distressingly apolitical character.

Success in such a venture will be aided by an understanding of the history and ongoing challenges of the civic engagement movement in higher education and the imperative to build on progress to date. It will also require serious attention to the reasons for young people's distaste for current political practices and the opportunities this provides to introduce them to an alternative set of practices rooted in the belief that politics need not be focused on divisive partisan politics and "sound bite" campaigns but rather myriad opportunities for citizens in all spheres to produce public goods.

Over the past two decades, American higher education has engaged in considerable soul-searching about its core purposes, particularly its responsibility to our democracy. The mission statements of many institutions assert that higher education ought to embrace the challenge of preparing an enlightened citizenry.[7] But how might colleges and universities go about promoting civic and political consciousness and what are the civic roles of the institutions themselves? Further, if civic engagement is such important work, why isn't more of it occurring? Several books and reports recently published with the support of the Kettering Foundation offer an expansive view of the current civic landscape and examine both theoretically and empirically the rich possibilities for fostering democratic deliberation and engagement at our institutions of higher learning and in our communities.

The impetus for recent efforts to advance the civic purposes of colleges and universities stems from several sources. By the 1990s, there were pervasive concerns over a withering of the common life, which Harvard political scientist Robert Putnam brilliantly captured in his image of Americans "bowling alone."[8] Political engagement sharply declined and mistrust in government grew. A rising chorus of critics argued that colleges and universities had become self-absorbed (and self-serving) Ivory Towers, disconnected from and fundamentally disinterested in pressing societal problems. Then-president of the Carnegie Foundation for the Advancement of Teaching, Ernest Boyer, summed up the situation by saying, "I have this growing conviction that what is needed [for higher education] is not just more programs, but a larger purpose, a larger sense of mission, a larger clarity of direction in the nation's life."[9]

This state of affairs prompted hundreds and finally tens of thousands of individuals to act, resulting in the emergence of a far-reaching civic engagement movement.[10] The dozens of new networks and organizations that formed resulted in the creation of Campus Compact. This presidential coalition dedicated to promoting civic and community engagement has grown from 3 members in 1985 to more than 1,200 in 2008, nearly a quarter of all colleges and universities.

---

[7]Christopher Morphew and Matthew Hartley, "Mission Statements: A Thematic Analysis of Rhetoric across Institutional Type," *Journal of Higher Education*, 77, no. 3 (2006): 456-471.

[8] Robert D. Putnam, "Bowling Alone," *Journal of Democracy* 6 (2006): 65-78.

[9]Ernest Boyer, "Creating the New American College," *The Chronicle of Higher Education* (March 9, 1994).

[10]Matthew Hartley and Elizabeth Hollander, "The Elusive Ideal: Civic Learning and Higher Education," in *Institutions of Democracy: The Public Schools*, eds. S. Fuhrman and M. Lazerson (Oxford: Oxford University Press, 2005), 252-276.

The focus of these efforts has evolved over time. Early civic engagement initiatives focused solely on encouraging students to become involved in the community through volunteerism or "public service," as it tended to be called. Later, in the 1990s, there were efforts to also link community-based activities with the curriculum through service learning. Many colleges and universities created centers for community partnership in order to work collaboratively with local agencies and groups and actively promote the revitalization of distressed communities. Despite this important work, a number of critics raised concerns about limitations of many service-focused efforts. Nary a service-learning conference convened without bemoaning the need to move beyond "service-learning 101" and grapple with their deep systemic roots. In 1999, a seminal conference cosponsored by the American Council on Education and Campus Compact led to the drafting of the Presidents' Declaration on the Civic Responsibility of Higher Education, which was signed by more than 500 college and university presidents. The document pointedly concludes that, "This service is not leading students to embrace the duties of active citizenship and civic participation.... We must teach the skills and values of democracy." In sum, what had emerged was an apolitical civic engagement.

One of the great champions of efforts to connect these efforts to democratic goals has been the Kettering Foundation. The *Higher Education Exchange* (*HEX*), established in 1994, has been an important venue for scholars and practitioners to debate and discuss the democratic purposes of higher education. The legacy of this journal is reflected in the thoughtful and thought-provoking book *Agent of Democracy: Higher Education and the HEX Journey*, edited by David Brown and Deborah Witte. This volume, the product of two years of workshops that drew together a group of contributors to *HEX*, offers clearheaded acknowledgement of the challenges attendant to this work. The American democracy faces what Kettering president David Mathews aptly characterizes as "megachallenges."

If America's great democratic experiment is not faltering, it is at least in need of reinvigoration. One of the most striking indicators is the political disengagement of America's youth and their disaffection with the political process. Trend data from the Higher Education Research Institute at UCLA, which surveys several hundred thousand students annually, shows the percentage of incoming freshmen who agreed that it is "important for me to keep up to date with political affairs" declining from around 60 percent in 1966 to 28 percent by 2000. The report from Abby Kiesa and colleagues at the Center for Information & Research on Civic Learning & Engagement (CIRCLE), *Millennials Talk Politics* offers important insights into the minds of 18- to 25-year-olds. At a time when volunteerism and local involvement has increased, students have grown increasingly ambivalent about politics. They see politics as dominated by polarized debate, with little room for compromise and nuance. They dislike "spin" and find it hard to imagine how to access a political system dominated by "big money." Politics is seen as "slow moving, as well as messy and hard to understand (23). Politicians are viewed as distant from the problems of their constituents. Voting is not considered as an effective way to bring about change—organized groups of people are. Students seek opportunities for open conversations about important issues that can help them decide their own point of view. But they often feel inundated by information, especially in the age of the inexhaustible Internet opportunities, and are uncertain what information to trust. The Kiesa study also shows that opportunities for civic engagement differ widely, depending upon the type of college. Underresourced colleges were much less likely to provide civic engagement opportunities for students.

Despite such concerns, many students are interested in finding ways to be involved, and this Millennial generation did participate in the 2004 national election which showed an 11 percent uptick in youth voting, the largest since 1992. Given pervasive discontent with the political system and uneven opportunities for civic engagement, Peter Levine, in *Agent of Democracy*, observes that "the spike in youth voting in 1992 gave way to a substantial turnout decline in 1996 and 2000. However, the rate of student volunteering increased just as turnout fell" (18). Surveys of participants in 47 focus groups found that most (64 percent) felt they could make some or a great deal of difference in their communities while nearly the same proportion (60 percent) indicated that the political system in the country is not responsive to the genuine needs of the public. How, then, can the democratic fires of our democracy be rekindled?

The Contested Civic Purposes of American Higher Education

Although the civic purposes of schooling have been widely touted (one can scarcely find a college mission statement or commencement address that doesn't espouse service to society and in many cases the fostering of an enlightened citizenry), civic language has often outstripped meaningful action. Perhaps it would be most accurate to say that our institutions of higher learning have increasingly found themselves faced with competing commitments. A recent Public Agenda study of parents' attitudes, *Squeeze Play: How Parents and the Public Look at Higher Education Today*, shows that many see college as "the only path to a good job," although many are worried about its availability because of cost" (2-3). It's no small wonder that professional majors outstrip liberal arts graduates at most colleges and universities. In the rush to establish credentials, other historical purposes of higher education, including civic engagement, have been lost in the shuffle. Increasingly, a college education has come to be seen as a private good—something individuals purchase to benefit themselves.

The follow-up study, *I'm Just Not That Into Politics: Public and Leadership Views on Higher Education and Civic Engagement*, on attitudes toward the purposes of college reinforces this view that college's primary role is to prepare students for the labor force. Education for civic engagement is viewed as a very low priority. This state of affairs has distorted the values and altered the behaviors of these institutions. Many institutions find themselves competing for students by engaging in a war of ever-increasing amenities. One senior admissions officer recently ruefully described being asked by a prospective student how tall the campus' climbing wall was. The punch line? The university rests at the foot of the Rockies. While a roommate dispute might be creatively conceived as an occasion to practicing the art of living in community, it can be a tough sell. In an essay in *Agent of Democracy*, Adam Weinberg, then Colgate University's Dean of the College explains: "A parent will call us because their son/daughter is being kept up by a roommate. We explain that this is a great opportunity for their son/daughter to learn how to get along with people and to negotiate space—a fundamental skill of democracy. A parent will respond by saying that they don't care about civic skills, they sent their child to college to get good grades so they can get a good job" (109).

Apathy toward a civic agenda is not just the result of external pressures; resistance can be found within the academy as well. The German research university model which gained ascendancy over the past century and a half has produced a system that rewards faculty members who publish in prestigious disciplinary journals rather than individuals who apply their scholarly gifts in partnership with community members in order to resolve pressing problems, what Ernest Boyer called the "scholarship of engagement."[11] The contributors to *Agent of Democracy* underscore the ways in which prevailing academic norms have become inimical to a civic imperative. Claire Snyder reminds us that although the American Social Science Association was founded as an agent of societal change, this transformational agenda quickly ran afoul of the desire to assert scientific "objectivity" and it became unworkable as broad areas of study fragmented into specializations such as sociology, political science, economics (63). This has had far-reaching effects. Even at liberal arts institutions that are dedicated to forming the minds and hearts of students, disciplinary norms prevail. As Weinberg observes, "Too many faculty have professionalized themselves. They see themselves as a narrow type of scientist.... Great civic education comes from faculty who think about themselves, their work, and their teaching in much more craftlike ways"(114). Political scientist and organizer Harry Boyte describes the "growing detachment of academia from public life"(84). He argues that public engagement offers an antidote for the tendency towards detached and all-too-neat abstract reasoning. "Public work politics is urgently needed to complicate every kind of abstract, categorical, idealized mode of thought. Such politics is rooted in the gritty soil of human plurality"(87). In sum, engagement is not only good for society; it adds deeper dimensions of analysis and understanding to academic work.

But such work remains marginal on many campuses. Conveying the findings of a focus group of engaged faculty at a land-grant university, Scott Peters notes that "many of them claimed that the work they do is not valued, supported, or pursued by most of their academic peers"(145). The approach flies in the face of accepted standards. A faculty member at another land-grant university observed: "I am always engaged in an internal dialog

---

[11] Ernest Boyer, "The Scholarship of Engagement," *Journal of Public Service and Outreach* 1 (1996).

in meetings like this one between what I hear around the table and what I know the dominant university culture is asking: where's the beef in validated research results?" (159-159). The civic engagement movement clearly faces some prodigious ideological barriers within the academy.

The external environment has also conspired to apoliticize the academy. Claire Snyder notes that the ascendancy of political liberalism has had a deleterious effect on our political system. In stark contrast to the individual activism espoused by civic republicanism "the liberal citizen has individual rights but few duties" (53). Further, many citizens (including young people) have concluded that powerful interest groups now dominate the political process, resulting in what Crenson and Ginsberg call a "downsizing of democracy."[12]

Finding a Way Forward

Despite the considerable challenges outlined above, these readings offer a measure of hope. They describe a variety of strategies that colleges and universities have enacted in order to advance their democratic purposes. The use of democratic dialogue as a promising practice for problem solving is the one that is most comprehensively addressed in these readings and one Kettering has played a leading role in promoting.

One of the richest examples comes from Katy Harriger and Jill McMillan of Wake Forest University. Harriger and McMillan detail the results of a four-year experiment with deliberative dialogue in their book *Speaking of Politics*. The authors recruited a group of 30 students who enrolled in 2 sections of a first-year seminar entitled "Deliberative Democracy." The student group also helped organize events promoting democratic dialogue on campus and in the community. The book describes how the project unfolded over the course of four years and measures the impact on the students involved, as well as the impact on students much less involved, and those not at all involved. The impacts on these 30 students were significant: it increased their understanding of politics, their sense of agency, their sense of responsibilities as citizens and it gave them skills useful to them as citizens

---

[12]Matthew A. Crenson and Benjamin Ginsberg, *Downsizing Democracy: How America Sidelined Its Citizens and Privatized Its Public* (Baltimore, MD: Johns Hopkins University Press, 2002).

and in their personal lives. There is even evidence that students who merely participated in one deliberation gained from the experience.

One of the benefits of this volume is that it honestly describes some of the challenges attendant to this work. For example, deliberations held in the community posed the most difficulty for students. Faculty struggled with how much guidance to give them. Also, although these faculty members aimed to create a diverse cohort of students, they were somewhat impeded by a predominantly wealthy and white student body. What makes this account so interesting and useful, however, is that Harriger and McMillan approach the initiative as an experiment and a work in progress. They recognize that faculty need to embrace new approaches to their work. They understand that "stronger, more eloquent, better informed community members will unfairly influence weaker participants" (23). Or, as Mary Stanley puts it in her critique of deliberation in *Agent of Democracy*, too great an insistence on "civility" can end up silencing voices deemed "disruptive" (31).

Despite such misgivings, the findings of the study suggest that designing learning experiences that emphasize democratic dispositions and behaviors can have a powerful effect on the experience of undergraduates. The experiment also is a promising antidote to the problem expressed in the *Millennials Talk Politics* report: that students find it hard to be informed about public issues and to sort through information conveyed through the popular media, often with a contentious partisan bent (5).

Deliberation & the Work of Higher Education: Innovations for the Classroom, the Campus, and the Community, edited by John Dedrick, Laura Grattan, and Harris Dienstfrey, ably describes the use of deliberation in a variety of contexts—at different kinds of institutions and in various academic programs. This volume demonstrates the rich possibilities of inviting students to engage in this work by grappling with pressing societal issues in the context of their academic experience. In some powerful examples, deliberation is coupled with course-based service learning. David Cooper at Michigan State University describes how the combination of service, community-based research and issue framing and dialogue facilitation in humanities classes at all levels can help deepen students' connections to the community and "move them from an awareness of issues into pragmatic problem-solving strategies" (137). Exposing students to deliberation also has the advantage of introducing them to a citizen-based movement to reclaim democratic life that is widespread at the local level but not generally recognized in national politics. As Dudley and Morse from Virginia Tech, tell us "the current environment of public service demands practitioners who work collaboratively with citizens for the public good" (165). Allison Crawford, a Wake Forest political science major, who was a Democracy Fellow, clearly articulates the impact of using her deliberative skills as part of a service-learning course. In working with a local community organization to organize dialogues about the local school system, she learned that the skills she had acquired could translate into meaningful solutions for real people (277-278).

Kettering's research has also been useful in rethinking the use of service-learning experiences to instill in students a sense of personal efficacy—"I can make a difference in my community." As Peter Levine notes in his essay in *Agent of Democracy*, the best examples of service learning are "true collaborations among students, professors, and community members; they have a political dimension (that is, they organize people to tackle fundamental problems collectively); they combine deliberation with concrete action; and they are connected to [teaching and learning outcomes]" (21). Of course, service-learning efforts often fall short of this ideal. This fact has tended to produce some rather unfortunate misconceptions regarding this useful pedagogy, some of which are reflected in these readings. Service learning is conflated with volunteerism or with well-meaning but ultimately palliative service, or with service *to* communities, rather than capacity building *with* communities. Given the burgeoning literature on service learning, which describes its applicability in addressing a variety of learning outcomes, including civic development, and its efficacy as a strategy for building long-term democratic partnerships between universities and communities, it is a shame that its potential is not explored in greater detail in these readings.

Looking Forward

What does the future hold? This is a time of great opportunity. As Peter Levine notes, the current generation of Millennials offers hope: "The early signs ... suggest a strong commitment to volunteer service matched by an increased interest in formal politics." Forty-seven percent of eligible 18- to 24-year-olds voted in 2004 (27). The Barack Obama presidential campaign shows how effectively young people can be mobilized by a message of constructive change, building across our differences, and pursuing nonconflict, nonideological approaches to solving real problems. This message has been combined with lots of opportunities for engagement through technological social networking mechanisms, which are widely used by young people. It will be important to nurture this rise in idealism and optimism.

To accomplish this, higher education needs to reclaim and reassert the democratic purposes of their civic mission and be clear about their goals. Penn State hosted two dozen colleagues in 2004 for a National Public Scholarship Conversation. However, Jeremy Cohen remarks: "Missing ... was a sustained consideration of democracy itself–either what it is or how to practice it" (160). Inherent in most of the Kettering material is a view of the democracy that is rooted in a Deweyan ideal of citizens practicing democracy in their neighborly communities through discussion and action. This view implies that the central task of teaching civics is not simply to understand how a bill becomes a law or to appreciate the responsibilities of the three branches of government but to help students understand how to create things of public value, whether on campus or off. This requires the development of civic skills, such as an ability to listen carefully to citizens as well as experts, to formulate and articulate a well-founded opinion or idea, and to weigh various policy alternatives. But to build these skills we need to contemplate an academy in which students are empowered (intellectually and practically) to challenge the status quo, including confronting authorities that reside on their own campus, an outcome that is rarely welcomed by administrators.

This view of democracy would also require a shift in faculty roles from acting as objective pundits or experts able to provide technical solutions to problems, to intellectuals who catalyze debate, develop relationships among diverse constituencies, act as coaches and are, themselves, part of the process of reinvigorating the public square. This is contrary to much of what occurs on many of our campuses today. As Scott Peters observes regarding land-grant institutions, "Instead of using a political language of public relationships ... the prevailing view employs a mechanical language of responsive public service that focuses on the provision of technical solutions" (124).

A democratic civic engagement would also have to take the role of the community much more seriously. Underlying the perspective represented by the writers reviewed here is a common belief that there is knowledge to be gained from the community as well as from the academy. Democracy is strengthened when each can learn from the other and apply both kinds of knowledge to seeking solutions to our most pressing problems. But truly reciprocal partnerships are difficult to establish. Many are, in the words of Mathews, a problematic "drop-in, drop-out, observe and advise relationship" (222). All of it, it is safe to say, is a "hard sell" for many faculty trained in traditional disciplines that stress expertise, privileges "objective, scientific" research and has as its highest value, replication of the next generation of scholars. To make things more difficult, community members may be reticent about establishing relationships where there has been a history of Ivory Tower aloofness, especially when it has been coupled with institutional expansion.

What we see in these readings, and in general in the field, are a host of worthy civic engagement activities. What is conspicuously absent is the purposeful, strategic integration of these efforts. What is required now are more comprehensive and orchestrated approaches to civic engagement that intentionally use a range of strategies in order to make a difference in the lives of students and communities, like the University of Charleston's efforts to radically redesign its undergraduate curriculum using many active learning approaches, including dialogue, as described by Douglas Walters in *Deliberation & the Work of Higher Education* (193-208). As envisioned at the outset of this essay, powerful civic education will be achieved when student experiences in and out of the classroom are consciously designed to provide myriad, different, but reinforcing, opportunities to gain civic knowledge and skills, including skills for "political" participation.

There is another element of civic engagement efforts that is too often missing. We live in a time when the "neighborly community" is increasingly international, as well as local, and a time when concepts of democracy are deeply challenged. Mary Stanley reminds us that the academy has an important role to play in bringing new ways of looking at "big issues" in our society. Stanley points out that all work, including "public work," is being transformed by a dedication to global efficiency, which trumps all other values. She calls for a "loud and proud" critical examination of practices and assumptions that support neoliberal globalization as a natural process.

Stanley's essay reminds us how little we ask students (and ourselves) to confront and challenge the status quo and how infrequently there are conversations in the civic engagement movement about deeply troubling issues like the Iraq war and the impact the "war on terror" is having on our democratic institutions both economically and constitutionally. One notable exception here is noted in Cohen's essay in *Agent of Democracy* in which his use of the war and its usurpation of constitutional rights as an example of why higher education must teach students about the theory and practice of democratic citizenship to fulfill the role posited by James Madison: to "throw that light over the public mind which is the best security against crafty and dangerous encroachments on the public liberty" (154). Indeed, Cohen's mention is noteworthy in being the singular discussion in all of these writings about issues of basic democratic freedoms, such as *habeas corpus*, freedom of speech, and rights to privacy, which have been influenced and even abrogated during this time of war.

In fact a number of campuses have begun focusing attention on the larger sociopolitical context in which these issues have emerged. The Ford Foundation president, Susan Berresford, along with 15 college presidents stated, in 2005 that they were "deeply troubled by reports of growing religious intolerance and of increasing restrictions on academic freedom on college and university campuses. In the wake of 9/11 and the continuing conflicts in the Middle East, the tone of academic debate has become increasingly polarized, and, in some cases, we see attempts to silence individuals, faculty and students alike, with controversial views. We believe that these problems are symptoms of the nation's larger and more complex challenge of sustaining informed political and civic discourse."[13] The Ford Foundation issued a request for proposal to colleges to undertake "Difficult Dialogues" on their campuses, and 675 responded. (There were only 27 grants available.) Some of the campuses that received grants proceeded to organize dialogues that involved community members as well as students, once again reinforcing the potential power of campus/community deliberation to address even our

---

[13] Susan Berresford, "Difficult Dialogues: Promoting Pluralism and Academic Freedom on Campus, a Letter from Higher Education Leaders and Susan Berresford to College and University Presidents" (New York: Ford Foundation, March 31, 2005).

most complicated pressing national and international issues with rigor not rancor.

Combining our best strategies for preparing our students for their role in a 21st-century democracy in a shrinking world is a complicated and pressing task, and we are still learning how to do it well. Toni Morrison reminds us how much is at stake if we do not find a way a way to persevere: "If the university does not take seriously and rigorously its role as guardian of wider civic freedoms, as interrogator of more and more complex ethical problems, as servant and preserver of deeper democratic practices, then some other regime or ménage of regimes will do it for us, in spite of us, and without us." [14]

Elizabeth Hollander
Tufts University

Matthew Hartley
University of Pennsylvania

---

[14] Toni Morrison, "How Can Values Be Taught in the University?" lecture delivered at the Center for Human Values, Princeton University (Princeton, NJ: April 27, 2000), found online at http://www.umich.edu/mqr/morrison.htm, accessed 3/5/2008.

CHAPTER TWO

Deliberation and the Civic Education of College Students

IN OVER 25 YEARS OF RESEARCH, Kettering has found that deliberation offers one of the most promising practices in the movement to strengthen and renew democracy. Deliberation allows citizens to experience a different kind of politics in which issues are named in their terms and they are the central actors. Kettering's recent research on the political attitudes of college students and the use of deliberation on college campuses suggests that deliberation may have an especially important role to play in the civic education of the next generation of citizens. These studies find that despite ambivalence toward politics as usual, young people are more eager than ever to engage in politics, and deliberation may offer students just the kind of transformative experience they are seeking.

Deliberation as part of a movement for citizen politics assumes that citizens are interested in and capable of taking part in political discussions. It is not meant for apathetic citizens, but rather for those who want to play an active role in ruling themselves but feel shut out of politics as usual. To test whether deliberation might make a difference in the political engagement of students in the current "Millennial" generation, we asked Abby Kiesa and her colleagues at the Center for Information & Research on Civic Learning & Engagement (CIRCLE) to talk to students about their attitudes toward politics. Based on survey and focus group data from campuses around the country, *Millennials Talk Politics* finds college students today to be deeply frustrated with politics, yet yearning for authentic spaces for meaningful political discussion.

IN 1993, the Charles F. Kettering Foundation published *College Students Talk Politics*.... The study found, among other things, that students considered politics "irrelevant" to their lives and saw little purpose in ever actively participating in the political system. We wanted to know whether and how college students' civic engagement had changed after almost 15 years of tumultuous political events and work by colleges and universities.... We spoke with undergraduates in focus groups on 12 four-year college and university campuses across the United States.

Today's College Students Are More Engaged than Generation X Was.... We found that students live in a different world from those who attended college in the early '90s.... Millennials are more involved in both civic and political life than their predecessors.... The students in our focus groups do not write off politics as irrelevant or unchangeable. By a ratio of almost eight to one, they say that government policies are relevant to the issues that concern them. In the words of a Maryland student: "If individuals themselves do something about issues that are actually about policy change, then nothing is going to be done." ... Many of these college students want to be involved and consider it important to participate, although often they do not know how to engage or doubt their ability to have a great deal of impact.

Millennials Are Involved Locally with Others but Are Ambivalent about Formal Politics. A large majority of college students are volunteering in a wide spectrum of areas (although some of the volunteering we perceive to be episodic).... When asked for the fundamental purpose or reason for their engagement activities, the most popular response is "to help others." A Maryland student says, "I think volunteering is beneficial because you take it upon yourself to go out and do something then and there."

Some students do prefer individual acts of service to politics. For instance, a student from Dayton says, "But in everything I have to do in a school day, the last thing I'm going to care about it politics.... I mean, I'd rather go and help that kid read." A New Mexico student says, "Like the government is like really far away and something that you can't really affect or change, but something that you can actually do in your community and see the results of might be more like motivating for people."

... In fact, students want to engage the political system, but largely find it inaccessible. A Wake Forest student says, "I just get this feeling about politics as this inaccessible realm that people don't really have that much participation in." Students also blame the politicians for the inaccessibility of the political system. They assert that because they lack the financial resources to contribute to political campaigns, politicians often turn a deaf ear to the college population. In focus groups, students readily discuss issues that concern them. Yet many students are not able to articulate how those policies are put into place and what levels of government have authority in a given area.... A New Mexico student says, "One thing that I guess kind of dissuades me from taking action is I guess I would call it impatience or just general frustration. If I join a group is it going to make a dent, is it going to make a difference? And it feels like it won't."

Millennials Dislike Spin and Polarized Debates and Seek Authentic Opportunities for Discussing Public Issues. Students perceive politics, as it currently exists, as always an "either/or" debate with no other options.... College students' aversion to joining a particular political party stems from the fact that they do not want to be limited in their personal beliefs by a party label.... Students feel if they subscribe to a particular party, then their beliefs will be confined to that party's platform. A Princeton student explains, "I'm trying to figure out what's right, what's wrong, what's ethically acceptable, and pulling my views from so many different places, it's hard to put myself into one particular part."

Contrary to popular belief, it is not lack of time that keeps some college students from following the news—roughly 1 in 10 participants say that a "lack of time" is a reason they are not informed. Instead, the focus group conversations suggest that students feel overwhelmed by the amount of information that is available to them. In the words of a Minnesota student, "There's definitely an information overload." ... One New Mexico student says, "There's just so much coming at you at once. Maybe when you're watching a TV show you hear people argue, argue, argue it's overwhelming, I guess."

... Additionally, a clear pattern is that focus group participants complain about the quality of the media. In their eyes, many media sources cannot be trusted because they present information with a partisan spin. A student from Wake Forest says, "I think politics is very shady. I don't think that you can trust what politicians say, but you can't really trust what the news says." ... A Dayton student says, "I want to know what's really going on. I don't want to know how someone feels about it. So then I could form my own opinion instead of hearing this skewed version of the truth."

... In contrast, we spent almost 100 hours in focus groups sitting with students talking about the political system and very few heated moments of conversation arose. A Kansas State student says, "I think that's why people don't feel like their voice matters, because rarely do we see discussions or something where you feel non-threatened and able to voice your opinion." A classmate adds, "I think it's too bad it's just a focus group. Why can't we just do this any time?" College students value such conversations and see them as a form of politics. In one of the focus groups at Tougaloo a student replies, "I think this discussion here could be considered a political act."

All Students Need to Have Opportunities for Civic and Political Participation and Students Need Opportunities and Space for Deliberation on Public Issues. ... Many of the problems that we identify in this report—for example, an overload of untrustworthy political information, confusion about formal political institutions, and uncertainty about how to achieve social change—could be mitigated if students had more opportunities to discuss current issues or had experiences that stimulated discussions. They especially need conversations that draw diverse participants and that are open and authentic, not dominated by people or organizations that have political agendas....

We believe that if students were given more opportunities to discuss current events, many would respond enthusiastically.... College students are hungry for a particular kind of conversation that is serious and authentic, involves diverse views, but is free of manipulation and spin. They want discussions that are open-ended in the sense that everyone is truly trying to decide what should be done. In short, we see evidence that there is substantial demand for deliberation on college campuses.

With a strong but inchoate desire for political engagement, turned off by partisan spin but seeking spaces for authentic discussion, college students are more desperate than ever for a new approach to civic education. This piece from David D. Cooper, Professor of Writing, Rhetoric, and American Culture at Michigan State University, comes from *Deliberation & the Work of Higher Education*, an edited volume of stories of innovative experiments in the use of deliberation to improve student learning and better prepare them for democratic citizenship. Cooper's contribution tracks a three-year experiment in which he incorporated deliberation into a four-course sequence, from a general education writing requirement to an elective upper division seminar in American studies. In the excerpt below Cooper tells the story of a student's experience in a capstone research project, then he offers personal reflections on the uses of deliberation to teach students that they can be "agents of democracy."

Arriving at the Senior Capstone

One advantage of using deliberative practices and active-learning techniques is that the impact of subject matter often ripples outside the classroom and beyond the usual tidy brackets of the semester calendar. That was certainly the case for Sarah W., one of the members of the Civic America seminar. After the semester was over, she asked whether I would direct her senior capstone requirement. Sarah wasn't particularly excited over the prospect of conducting a research project and writing a senior paper. She lit up, however, when I suggested, "Why don't you do a full-blown public forum on the study circle topic 'Who Is College For?' in our Civic America seminar last semester?"

Sarah hit the ground running. All I did was help connect her to the right campus and community networks and meet with her regularly to help keep her on track....

"This event," Sarah wrote in a press release, "will give participants a rare opportunity to discuss the issue and work toward a common solution. It is not going to be a debate. Rather, it will be a chance to converse about an important issue that touches all of us, work toward understanding all viewpoints, and suggest some solutions." She was right. On April 12, 2005, Sarah held a small but successful deliberative campus forum on "Who Is College For?"

Afterward, Sarah submitted a bulging portfolio that chronicled her experience with the deliberative forum.... Here are some excerpts:

> ... I went into this project blind, but I have come out feeling confident that if ever asked to do something like this again in my life, I will be able to use the skills I learned over this semester....
>
> The deliberative process is something that has become almost foreign to our society. People want to debate issues, not discuss them. Living in a democracy, it is so important that citizens are educated about their options when it comes to deciding where they stand on issues.... The participants walked in with one or two opinions, and left having learned to both form new opinions and to change their existing opinions. More importantly, they were able to listen to the opinions of others and witness democracy at work.... This was an experience that I will look back on as being something that helped me to break out of my norm and learn new skills, while also impacting my community. I am really proud of my project, and I will always value the lessons I learned through this experience.

Some Postcards Home

I've come through these four seasons of deliberative learning with many more lessons, insights, and future challenges than I have the space to recount here. I briefly note the most important among them:

One of the things I most admire about the NIF-style of public deliberation and its adaptability to the humanities classroom is the way it respects and elevates personal experience in the calculus of public problem solving.... I am always amazed at how powerful personal stories can be and how essential they are to public creation.... The reciprocity between what people care about deeply and passionately and the hard work of hammering out the political will it takes to get people acting together is the greatest asset and the most daunting challenge of deliberative learning....

The same thing happens in a good personal essay.... It's interesting to me that NIF-style public forums are another discursive arena where story, voice, and personal presence matter. In this sense, *narrative* connected my work as a literary editor and my experiments in public conversation and deliberation in the undergraduate classroom....

By helping students learn to become better interpreters of their own lives, society, and culture, my home disciplines of rhetoric and American studies—indeed, the humanities-at-large—can become durable and enduring resources for democracy.... The humanities' quest to find truth and knowledge, as English professor Maria Farland has observed, often originates in problems or challenges that should rightly be considered "public business," especially when that knowledge yields moral insight and ethical clarity or purpose into such pressing issues as mapping the human genome, preserving the natural environment, cloning controversies, reining in youth violence, balancing individual rights and social responsibilities in the wake of 9/11, and resolving racial tensions in our communities and schools—all legitimate terrain of humanistic inquiry and insight. In short, humanists can serve the public interest by sharing their deep understanding of the roots of public problems in ways that speak to everyday experience. To fulfill that legacy, the humanities professoriate must do a better job of closing the gap between the world of ideas and the theoretical reflexes that animate faculty culture, on the one hand, and our students' preference for concrete applications of knowledge and for active methods of learning, on the other. We need to find new and more effective ways of aligning pedagogical techniques and practices so they better address the disconnect between action and ideas that, for better or worse, characterizes the current generation of undergraduates' predominant learning style and their practices of citizenship. Such pedagogical techniques and practices include the use of active and interactive teaching and learning practices, especially the deliberative pedagogy I experimented with, where the learning ethos of the classroom—syllabus construction and management, assignments, assessment, heuristics, architecture, everything—is modeled after a public forum, and my role as teacher becomes that of a moderator and my students become agents and participants in the productive public work of the course. We also need to better integrate into the curriculum active research opportunities for undergraduates—as in Sarah's capstone—instead of using the undergraduate classroom as a site where we download our research expertise. Students need to be viewed as active producers of knowledge and agents of democracy and not primarily as passive consumers of information. Above all, we have to attend to those features and flaws of the campus culture and its disciplinary arrangements that are detrimental to civic involvement— for example, the degree to which uncontested skepticism is valued and rewarded, the absence of idealism, or the disconnect between the university's professed "mission" and its actual relationship and behavior toward the surrounding community. The same call to urgency, consequence, responsiveness, and relevance that John Dewey issued to the discipline of philosophy 100 years ago applies even more so today to American studies, rhetoric, and the liberal arts generally. "Better it is for philosophy to err in active participation in the living struggles and issues of its own times," Dewey insisted, "than to maintain an immune monastic impeccability without relevancy and bearing in the generating of ideas of its contemporary present."

All too often, deliberation in the civic education of college students receives limited institutional support, resulting in sporadic experiments with little impact. However, in *Speaking of Politics*, Katy J. Harriger and Jill J. McMillan from Wake Forest University describe the results of the Democracy Fellows Program, which integrated deliberation into the curriculum in classroom, campus, and community settings for a cohort of students over a four-year period. Despite a critical and realistic sense of the limits of deliberation, the study provides strong evidence that students who experience deliberation are more likely to be engaged in politics and to see themselves as civic actors.

IN THE FALL SEMESTER OF 2001, we began a journey that would take us through four years of experimentation with deliberative democracy in a campus setting with 30 entering first-year students. We called the group "Democracy Fellows," and we worked with them in the classroom, on campus, and in the wider community as we explored together the joys, the challenges, and just plain hard work that come with democratic processes.

For several decades, scholars and practitioners have been concerned about the decline of political, and more broadly, civic engagement among U.S. citizens. Declining voter turnout, polls showing alienation from public life and cynicism about politics and politicians, and evidence of significant lack of knowledge of, and interest in, politics have all raised concerns about the health of American democracy. While adults tend to feel anger toward politics, work in the 1990s showed that younger voters felt pessimistic and disconnected. More recent data indicate a slight upswing, suggesting that perhaps this trend has bottomed out and a new generation of "millennial" students may be developing more interest in politics in the aftermath of September 11, 2001.

[We] began our experimentation with deliberation in the classroom. Here, we asked ourselves whether the classroom is a microcosm of the larger political landscape or a venue for change. Is it possible to appropriate the best of deliberation, use it to teach students another means of political discourse, and allow it to work the "transformative" magic which its advocates claim? Our [initial] seminar focused on the theory and practice of deliberation. We began by exploring democratic theory about citizens' role in a democracy and the importance of public talk. We then taught the students how to deliberate through three deliberations in which we served as the moderators. We followed the [National Issues Forums] model for these deliberations using NIF issue books that focused on public education, race and ethnic tensions, and the role of the university in promoting civic engagement.

Classroom deliberation enabled students to "enact" both the knowledge about political and deliberative theory they had learned and to practice it. Furthermore, the classroom offer[ed] a "safe" environment where the consequences of stumbling are far less than they are in the "real" world. One student, who had entered the program with a good deal of skepticism about politics, wrote: "… I have received the opportunity to realize how deliberation can transform an apathetic, disenchanted public into an active, engaged citizenry. The possibility of this vision truly excites me."

Despite the obvious learning advantages of the classroom setting, we found that classrooms are unable to simulate an authentic democratic environment and discussion. When we talked with the students about their frustrations in coming to action, they identified their lack of power to influence decision makers. One young woman wrote that "there were several issues [where] we, as students, felt that we had no control over the problem, and therefore had little motivation to act."

Once democratic skills are developed, it is important to test them in that larger world, and as our students moved from the classroom to a wider world the challenges of using these newfound skills became progressively harder and more "real." During the final month of the first-year seminar, the Democracy Fellows worked in groups to identify issues that might lend themselves well to a campus deliberation. They chose to investigate what they perceived to be the lack of a sense of community on campus among diverse groups of students and between students, faculty, administration, and the city of Winston-Salem.

Given the well-documented fact that college students feel little sense of political efficacy, by far the most encouraging result of bringing deliberative training to the campus was the empowerment of students who experienced deliberation directly, in contrast with those who had not. When a student-initiated, student-led forum succeeded in gathering 120 individuals from the university's major constituencies and generating ideas that were eventually translated into administrative policy changes, the shift in power, at least for a time, did not go unnoticed. In the course of the discussion, there was movement toward agreement that the issue as laid out in the issue book, was indeed problematic. Agreement increased by about 20 percent that the isolation of students from the wider community, lack of school spirit, and separation of campus groups were matters of concern. One student participant summed up the attitude change: "I felt encouraged to be more active. This strongly encouraged me to do things through my organization." And indeed that is what happened. Not only did students begin to discuss and enact suggestions from the deliberation, but, as noted earlier, members of the administration and student-life department took note as well.

If the campus deliberation allowed students to stay safely inside their bubble, the community deliberation clearly burst it, forcing them outside the protection of their teachers and friends into the local community that surrounded them. Here they had to participate face-to-face with people often very unlike themselves and deal with hard, often intractable, issues that stretched students' minds by their complexity. On October 2, 2003, the community deliberation on the subject of urban sprawl in Winston-Salem was held at SCIWORKS, a community science museum, and was attended by approximately 50 people. After a welcome and a short film on urban sprawl, attendees were broken into four groups, moderated, recorded, and timed by Democracy Fellows.

Not only were students forced from their comfort zones, which many of them recognized was valuable, but their awareness of the problems with urban sprawl increased dramatically. The town/gown divide, which characterizes almost every college town, also plagues Winston-Salem, but Democracy Fellows truly believed that they had taken at least a small step toward fracturing the dividing wall by the hard work they had done on behalf of the community. On the other hand, they found their administrative and planning skills inadequate to the task; their networks small and ineffective; their publicity strategies woefully lacking. And most critically, the students perceived that the community had stereotyped them as privileged college students who were doing "a little project" and were in over their heads.

Despite the commonalities of the students [in the class of 2001] when they entered college, those who learned and practiced deliberation for four years were qualitatively different from their classmates who did not.

- Democracy fellows were more involved in the traditional venues of political action that predict political involvement. The typical Wake Forest student could be substituting service for civic action, which many have feared, while Democracy Fellows developed a wider, more expansive political repertoire.
- Democracy Fellows were more attuned to the responsibilities of active citizenship. What stands out is their frequent use of the words *action* or *engagement*. Though they too struggled with the differences between what they often called "technical" versus "good" citizenship, it is clear that for them, *citizenship* came to mean "doing something" about politics.
- Democracy Fellows were more analytical and critical of political processes and their role in them. Shortly after the first-year seminar experience, we began to notice what we call "sophistication" in the way these students thought and talked about politics. They spoke of "developing an open mind," "giving serious thought to specific ways that I can get involved," "becoming public-minded."
- Democracy Fellows were more efficacious in their political attitudes and language.
- Democracy Fellows were more communal in their political language and outlook.
- Democracy Fellows were more imaginative in recognizing possibilities for deliberation and applying deliberative knowledge and skills to a broad range of situations.

Allison N. Crawford, a graduate of the Wake Forest program, recently wrote on the role of deliberation in the development of her political engagement. Her reflections were published in the volume, *Deliberation & the Work of Higher Education*.

ONE OF THE MOST FULFILLING of these classes [outside her academic majors] was a course I took my last semester at Wake Forest, "Introduction to Sculpture."... It is probably not a coincidence that the piece I created involved politics.

Driving around Winston-Salem prior to the 2004 presidential election and seeing campaign signs plastered everywhere gave me the idea of using campaign yard signs as my material of choice....

My project was an installation of signage and frames set in the grass outside of the campus's arts building....

... Someone remarked that seeing the piece forced us to talk about politics, a subject that people often try to avoid in discussion.... Would I have created such a piece had I not been a Democracy Fellow? Maybe not....

I know that working with the Democracy Fellows for four years helped foster important participatory civic skills.... Organizing a community forum and working as a group to accomplish a challenging task has proven to me that students can solve problems that have an impact on them and are willing to work with others to do so. In fact, I saw this often on my campus, where students banded together to start organizations, raise money, and donate their time and talents to problems ranging from AIDS in Africa to racial tensions on campus.... While I do not agree with the political views and ideas of all of the Democracy Fellows, I continue to respect and learn from them. Now we can have civil conversations on sensitive issues, and we can work together to solve tough problems.

One of the most difficult challenges facing these experiments is in ensuring that the experience of deliberation translates into skills that are meaningful outside of the classroom. In this interview, David Brown asks Joni Doherty, Director of the New England Center for Civic Life at Franklin Pierce University, to reflect on her experience as a teacher and practitioner of deliberation with college students. Doherty speculates on the far-reaching potential of experiences in deliberative democratic politics to impact the personal, professional, and civic lives of college students.

Brown: When reflecting on your deliberative experiences in the classroom you learned to put aside being a "sage on the stage" and instead becoming a "guide on the side." Is that what more academics should learn to do?

Doherty: One size that fits all just doesn't apply here. There are different teaching styles and learning styles. The important consideration is how best to engage students with the material. Someone who is comfortable with using the "sage on the stage" approach might think about how to engage students more interactively at some points during the class session without giving up lecturing, particularly if those lectures are passionately and effectively delivered. And even though I characterize myself as a "guide on the side" I still use mini-lectures to create some scaffolding for students to continue building on.

Another way to think about this is to consider not what the instructor is doing, but on what is happening with students. For example, you might focus on how well they retain what they are being taught. How well are they remembering and *using* what was presented in lecture? Exams measure a moment in time, but engaging them in speaking and doing (for example, through deliberative dialogue and civic engagement activities) will help them to conceptualize and to integrate knowledge and skills. So although not all academics are cut out to be the guide on the side, it is important for anyone interested in teaching effectively to carefully consider the many different practices available to us.

Brown: Your "ground rules for classroom deliberation" make the distinction between "dialogue" and "debate." How can students be helped in learning the difference between the two?

Doherty: A role-playing exercise called the 3Ds (for debate, discussion, and deliberation) is a very effective way of raising awareness about the different modes of communication. Pairs of students are asked to respond to a question using one of the modes while the rest of the group observes them. The question for the role-play should not be a controversial one because that will distract from focusing on process. One of our favorites is, "The provost has decided to send the two of you on a month-long trip anywhere in the world, all expenses paid. The only condition is that you both must travel and remain together during that month. Please (debate, discuss, deliberate) in order to select a destination."

Students readily identify that debate is about winning—scoring points through identifying weaknesses in the "opponent's" argument—and that it is valuable for clearly delineating differences in positions. Debaters often acknowledge that they play to the audience. It certainly is the role-play that evokes the most laughter.

Discussion, on the other hand, is about building relationships and accommodating the other person. Its goal tends to be focused on achieving harmony, which sometimes causes one to withhold opinions so as not to offend the other. This might work in the short-term but most students note that it eventually leads to resentment. Yet early on it can be quite effective for establishing and building relationships. However, this is not a spectator sport, like debate. The prioritizing of the interpersonal between the two participants during discussion, along with its sometimes meandering nature, leads the "audience" to note that they feel left out or bored while observing this role-play.

Brown: And then there is deliberation ...

Doherty: During the role-play of deliberation students are mentally participating as they observe, weighing the various options in their own minds. The students who are doing the role-play tend to ask questions in order to learn more about each other and the proposed destinations. Both subjective and objective considerations are more systematically identified and weighed. Interestingly, in my experience it has been the only role-play in which, in addition to the student's own desires, factors such as responsibility to the school or social justice issues are introduced.

After the exercise, everyone is asked to identify what they have noticed in terms of content and interpersonal dynamics, including body language, and to think about the effect on the audience. The goal is for students to realize that each mode of communication is most valuable when consciously selected to suit the context and goals of a particular situation. Just as you wouldn't use a screwdriver with nails or a hammer with screws, it's important to select the right communication tool for the task at hand.

Setting aside time to reflect together on how we are communicating with each other is time well spent in any course that uses discussion as a pedagogical tool. Students become much more conscious of the moments when the dynamic in the classroom shifts from learning to winning, shuts people down, or wanders off topic. It keeps all of us focused and aware of what is going on (or not) during our time together.

Brown: Do you find less acrimony among those engaged in deliberative dialogue?

Doherty: Absolutely. First of all, it's hard to be acrimonious when you are sitting in a circle face to face with those with whom you may disagree. People are not pigeonholed by their positions, but are instead understood as individuals with particular experiences and values. The period in which people share their personal connections with the issue deepens that sense of having a relationship with everyone present. Finally, the issue framework, which has three approaches for addressing the issue, assures that multiple perspectives will be considered and that we have not come together to pit one particular side against another.

Brown: Your "ground rules" also ask students to "speak from direct experience, not hearsay." With younger students, is that easier said than done?

Doherty: Actually it is easier done than not. Many first-year students are preoccupied with their personal lives and opinions. Some of this is developmental, some due to the challenges associated with the transition from high school to college. Whenever I can connect course content to their present and past experiences, they become much more engaged in learning. What had seemed remote or abstract becomes alive, the stuff of everyday life. These concrete experiences are incredibly helpful in moving students from broad generalizations to more careful analysis of specific instances, and to help them connect private concerns with the public realm.

For example, during one of the forums we held on energy one student stated that since her parents paid for the gas for her car, the issue didn't affect her personally. Yet as she gradually realized how deeply fuel costs impacted the lives of several other students in the room, she became much more concerned and was instrumental in identifying a number of actions that could be taken to conserve resources. Since many of our students are from the Northeast, most do not see immigration as an issue that affects them. However, many of their grandparents, and some of their parents, are immigrants and so we encourage them to share family stories. Next, we explore other connections, including how some students' families have saved money by hiring immigrants to do jobs such as landscaping or roofing or how some students have competed with immigrants for summer jobs. An issue that on first glance appeared quite remote has now become much more immediate and complex, particularly for those whose families have immigrated to America.

If personal connections aren't made, forums either can be painfully quiet affairs or coldly analytical. Conversely, students can withdraw if they care very much about an issue but don't see how they can make a difference. Instead of saying, "I'm overwhelmed!" they can appear not to care. I remember one particular forum on Democracy's Challenge where this happened. Many of the students did in fact care very much about the issue but didn't feel as though they could make a difference. They felt powerless and so mentally checked out.

Brown: Harriger and McMillan concluded that their "Democracy Fellows" 4-year program, which involved 30 students, made a difference for those participating. Do you think there is room in an institution's offerings to enlarge the student numbers for deliberation across the curriculum?

Doherty: The question assumes that it is necessary to make additions to the curriculum, which is not necessarily the case. I believe the question really should be about how best to engage students in the content. Integrating deliberative pedagogies into existing courses is one way to do that.

Brown: Harriger and McMillan concluded that the classroom is "ill designed to be an authentic democratic site, to connect the academic and 'real world,' and to move easily from talk to action." Would you agree?

Doherty: I agree it is difficult to move from talk in the classroom to action in the "real world." I know several of my colleagues here believe that is very important to identify and implement specific actions following deliberation and if that doesn't occur, they believe the deliberation falls short of its objectives. Certainly that is typically true in the community at large. However, action doesn't only mean that a specific policy is implemented or changed. For example, having students convene and lead a forum builds the convenors' and moderators' sense of agency and provides other students with an opportunity to practice deliberation. And everyone becomes more aware of the issue and the array of possible approaches for addressing it. It's educational action —building capacity for thoughtful civic engagement through the cultivation and development of the necessary commitment, knowledge, and skills. This kind of "action" is appropriate for all of the disciplines, not just the general education courses or political science or women's studies. After all, what profession doesn't have its ethical dilemmas? What profession is isolated from the public realm?

Brown: When you have noted a "sense of agency," does this underscore David Mathews's observation that the major contribution of deliberative forums "has been to give people an experience of what democratic politics can be like and what citizens can do"? How is it that students might develop a sense of agency from an experience that at first glance seems removed from the "real world"?

Doherty: I find it curious that so many people make a distinction between college and the "real world." First, there are more than two worlds! And second, students, faculty, and staff in the college world certainly experience their lives as "real." Although most, but not all, students are not yet responsible for supporting themselves or raising a family, they encounter many of the challenges faced by anyone who is living in relationship with other people. Not only are there an array of new personal and professional relationships, but there is the day-to-day work of creating and maintaining a larger community within and between all the various groups that are part of any campus. This is the way politics functions in our everyday lives in the "real world."

What David Mathews has observed about community forums is also true for campus-based and even classroom-based forums. Further, not only does it give students the experience of what democratic politics can be like, but many of them then take those deliberative practices and apply them to other situations. Just recently one of our civic scholars was asked to assist the Law Club in running an open forum with the local police chief regarding recent conflicts. He was invited to do so because some of the club members had attended a deliberative forum and thought it would be more effective. Another student told me that she used the listening skills she acquired as a civic scholar to successfully achieve full funding for one of our campus diversity clubs. It had received minimum funding since its inception. After she was able to hear—and thereby fully understand— the budget committee's concerns, she was able to effectively address them. Students have told me that it influences how they interact with each other. They are much more aware of how we communicate with each other and of what can be done to ensure that the exchanges are both honest and respectful.

Brown: Harriger and McMillan took deliberation out of the classroom to the larger campus. Their students acknowledged that they have "limited power and influence" on campus issues that mattered to them. Isn't this a handicap that is unavoidable? Isn't this also a handicap for graduates in the "real world"?

Doherty: We all have limited power and influence. Recognizing this is in itself powerful in that it can open us up to connecting with others. To act alone as an individual, or even in a particular group, is perpetually insufficient, particularly with regard to public issues that require ethical decisions. In this diverse global environment we are all part of a much larger and very complex network of other people who have differing life experiences, beliefs, and priorities. This is exactly why it is so important to be able to communicate effectively across differences. The work of building and maintaining vibrant and equitable communities is continuous, and requires continuous effort. This requires a kind of communication that values listening as well as speaking.

Brown: You put a premium on good "listening," which you say is "a skill that is not emphasized enough in education, or in our culture overall." Why is that?

Doherty: We live in a competitive society. We live in a culture that encourages each of us to focus on personal success. We are conditioned to "speak our minds" and assert and defend our individual opinions. Too often differences are seen as problematic. We are threatened if someone disagrees with us. We seek to win them over, to convince them of their error.

At a conference earlier this year, Parker Palmer, one of the presenters, brought up the idea of hospitality and it's stayed with me. It might seem like an odd or old-fashioned concept in our competitive society. It implies trust, safety, and kindness. For those concerned with academic rigor, it can sound like dumbing down course content or pandering. But let's consider why this idea sounds so out of place. According to Jane Tompkins, author of *Life in School: What the Teacher Learned*, faculty operate in an academic context that is often isolated through too-busy schedules, competition for resources, and the "absence of a culture of conversation." She writes, "If the places that young people go to be educated don't embody the ideals of community, cooperation, and harmony, then what people will learn will be the behavior these institutions do exemplify: competition, hierarchy, busyness, and isolation."

How rare it is that a differing view is seen as enriching or interesting. And yet that is just the attitude we need to have if we are to really listen to others, to open ourselves up to another perspective, to withhold judgment. Just think of what we could each learn from others if the art of listening was more valued in our culture. And it might help us all slow down and enjoy each other more. And that would certainly enrich our civic life too.

Brown: Is your assumption that students have to be educated for civic life, that it is an acquired trait, not an inherent one?

Doherty: Civic life exists and we are all part of it, whether we are aware of it or not. I don't see it as a trait, but as a dynamic comprised of layers of relationships. Some students are more civically aware and/or engaged while others are less so. In addition, there are many different ways of being involved with civic life beyond the more traditional service-oriented or advocacy-based activities.

The majority of students identify a college education as something that is essentially professional training for future careers. It's helpful to remind them that a liberal arts education can do more than simply provide workforce training (although it needs to do that too). Colleges have the responsibility to expand and deepen students' awareness of the complexity and richness of the world and their capacity for critical thinking and personal reflection. Doing so will ensure graduates are more aware of their own humanity and their connections to others. Even if a person leads an essentially private life with no apparent role in the public realm, one should understand that actions impact others far beyond that private inner circle of family and friends.

Brown: Do you think your work leads to "a different kind of politics"?

Doherty: I think of politics as relationships between people. There are personal politics and public politics and plenty of places where the two intersect. It is the action of figuring out how to relate to others in ways that are equitable and just. Being able to communicate respectfully and honestly allows for the open exchange of beliefs, experiences, and ideas that is essential for realizing this ideal. I believe the effort to do so is worthwhile because it enriches life and learning, whatever the field of academic study and wherever we live.

CHAPTER THREE

Public Scholarship: Academic Professionals Engaged in Democratic Work

NOWHERE IN OUR SOCIETY is the tension between democracy and expertise more evident than in academic scholarship. Although higher education professionals play an important social role as scholars in the development of state-of-the-art knowledge, this role requires expertise that is available only to a select few. The professional routines of academic scholarship (such as advanced training, specialized research, and publication for select audiences) tend to isolate scholars from society. At the same time, these routines make the work of scholars obscure, irrelevant, or alienating from the perspective of citizens. Whether in disseminating information to laity or providing services to consumers, the dominant modes of scholarship treat experts rather than citizens as the primary actors in addressing public problems. However, in this context new forms of scholarship are emerging which involve collaboration with active self-ruling citizens and redefine the role of expertise in democracy. The works excerpted here argue that this public scholarship project requires critical thinking about the disconnect between scholarship and the agency of citizens, and a new epistemology that affirms a role for citizens in advancing knowledge along with experts.

Since 1994, Kettering's *Higher Education Exchange*, edited by David Brown and Deborah Witte, has provided a forum in which scholars began questioning the politics of conventional forms of expertise, and a movement toward public forms of scholarship began to take shape. Jay Rosen's essay in a 1997 exchange with Alan Wolfe is one of the most eloquent early statements of the core values of public scholarship. Rosen, on the faculty of the Arthur L. Carter Journalism Institute at New York University, argues for scholarship done with citizens rather than for them, in which inquiry is social, cooperative, and relevant to communities.

IN A 1932 ESSAY, "The Scholar in a Troubled World," Walter Lippmann pointed to a "special uneasiness which perturbs the scholar." On the one hand, the student of human affairs "feels that he ought to be doing something about the world's troubles, or at least saying something which will help others to do something about them." On the other hand, "the voice of another conscience," that of the scholar, urges "a quiet indifference to the immediate and a serene attachment to the processes of inquiry and understanding." While Lippmann acknowledged the lure of engagement—and, indeed, succumbed to it in his own career—in 1932 he came down on the side of "quiet indifference." His reasoning is instructive. At "the point where knowledge is to be applied in action, there is a highly variable and incalculable factor." This factor is "public opinion," which Lippmann held in rather low esteem.

I'm reminded of these thoughts of Lippmann's in forming a reply to Alan Wolfe's wise and challenging essay, "The Promise and Flaws of Public Scholarship." In Wolfe's view, the scholar has no business trying to improve the people who are the public, or to "engage them round the clock" in deliberations they may not want or need. This is not respect, says Wolfe. It is condescending, or worse, manipulative. Respect to Wolfe means two things: first, accept the public and its views for what they are, not as we wish them to be; and then, speak truth to the public—and simultaneously to power. The kind of truth he has in mind comes with patient study, scrupulous data, clear writing, and the determination to be heard. This Wolfe says, is good scholarship, the kind we need.

"Public" for me implies something different than it does for Wolfe. A public scholar is neither a scold nor a servant of the polity. He or she is in the business of inquiry: trying to learn something that is hard to learn without investigation, patience, and a commitment to truth-telling, including the hard truths that polities and politicians may wish to avoid. But instead of seeing inquiry as a solitary venture, or a professional mission undertaken with academic colleagues, or the sort of truth-on-demand that policymakers expect from their hired hands, the public scholar views the work to be done as "public" work.

This means a number of things: first, the scholar's work is made to be shared with others outside the professional domain of academic inquiry; second, the quest to know originates in some problem or challenge that could usefully be called "public" business; third, the others with whom one is inquiring are not limited to experts, policy professionals, academics, or government officials seeking technical advice, but may include all manner of people: neighborhoods trying to build their capacity to work together and achieve common aims; journalists seeking a stronger civic identity; communities facing mounting problems that require people to deliberate and cooperate in novel ways; parents, teachers, administrators, students, and concerned citizens wondering why the latest "fix" failed to solve the problems of their schools; police departments and the people they're pledged to serve who want safer streets but no longer believe they can be bought with budgets; librarians who want public libraries to gain a more vital role in the life of the community.

To be sure, we need people who can withdraw to a life of serious contemplation, and return with advanced forms of understanding by which scholarly knowledge develops. We need civic spirited intellectuals like Alan Wolfe, who feel they owe the public their best estimate of what's happening and why. But we also need people ready for a different kind of work—done not *for* the public or its elected officials, but *with* people who are trying to become a public, a community able to know in common what its members cannot know alone and to imagine the possibilities their democracy may yet afford.

Although the specialization of professions and the development of technical knowledge are clearly necessary to address social problems, it nevertheless constitutes the central dynamic that disables citizen self-rule. In this selection from an essay in *Agent of Democracy*, Harry C. Boyte provides a vivid understanding of the logic of expertise and its consequences for democratic politics. Based on his work at the University of Minnesota and his experience in the civil rights movement, Boyte argues for transforming the role of academic expertise from the dominant paradigms of service delivery and dissemination of information to a democratic practice of building civic capacities in the tradition of community organizing.

PUBLIC WORK POSITS the citizen as the responsible and foundational agent of democracy—democracy's cocreator, not simply a voter, volunteer, customer, or protestor who demands his or her fair share of the goods. Democracy is not mainly elections, laws, and institutions but a society, a lived cultural experience....

Higher education takes on many roles in such a democracy. Our institutions are its "agents and architects," as Elizabeth Hollander and I put it in *The Wingspread Declaration* on the civic mission of research universities. They are not simply its researchers, critics, service providers, or the educators of its future leaders. Scholars, in turn, are engaged public figures, part of the world. Their work is not only to analyze and critique but also to stimulate conversations, to expand the sense of the possible, and to activate broader civic and political energies.

Redefining higher education's role in these terms is crucial in the early 21st century. Higher education is the premier knowledge institution in an era of exploding knowledge and knowledge technologies. It creates knowledge and it also credentials knowledge. It generates and diffuses conceptual frameworks that structure practices of all sorts, from global finance to parent education. It trains and socializes professionals....

If our institutions become infused with a renewed sense of democratic prophetic purpose, they will also help build flourishing democratic societies. The chief obstacle, in my view, is an opposing technocratic politics rooted in higher education. Technocratic politics—domination by experts removed from a common civic life—has spread throughout contemporary society like a silent disease. It is largely a politics without a name, presenting itself as an objective set of truths, practices, and procedures. Technocratic politics turns groups of people into abstract categories. It decontextualizes "problems" from the civic life of communities. It privatizes the world and creates cultures based on a philosophy of scarcity. It profoundly erodes the subjective experience of equal respect.

Public work counters the impersonal, abstract, decontextualized culture of technocracy and its associated left versus right politics. At the molecular level of everyday experience, public work brings back a view of politics as about negotiating the plural, grounded, sometimes conflicted but also relational qualities of the human condition in order to solve problems. At a somewhat larger level of analysis it recasts professional work as a public craft, with experts "on tap, not on top," to use the organizing phrase....

... Despite the democratic potential of knowledge, the explosion of knowledge and knowledge producing institutions has reinforced existing hierarchies and created new ones.

Technocracy's political qualities are hidden behind a stance of being "apolitical."...

"... We all have to follow the lead of specialists," wrote Walter Lippmann at the end of World War I.... Science was the model for liberal thinking; technocrats the model actors....

This pattern came to mean that academic knowledge produced by credentialed experts is what "counts," and the authority of those without formal credentials is systematically undermined. It detached professionals from the life of communities and eroded the civic cultures of organizations they direct. As citizens became clients and consumers, the process hollowed out the civic muscle of mediating institutions, from local unions to civically grounded schools, businesses, and voluntary associations. This dynamic has been a key reason for citizens' feelings of powerlessness....

When Edwin Fogelman and I interviewed senior faculty at the University of Minnesota in 1997 and 1998, we heard both about this detachment and its consequences. Leading faculty, from different disciplines, said that they consciously avoid mention of their public interests—what had led them into academia in the first place—for fear it might jeopardize their reputations for "rigorous scholarship." They feel increasingly cut off from local communities, or even their departmental communities, focused more on disciplinary or subdisciplinary reference groups....

In the first instance, the politics of public work builds on a tradition of theory and practice that has sought in recent decades to retrieve citizen-centered politics against the appropriation of politics by experts....

... In citizen-centered terms, politics is primarily the free, horizontal interactions among equal citizens, and only secondarily their vertical relationships with politicians or the state. Citizen-centered politics disputes the expert takeover of political life....

Secondly, the politics of public work confounds the separation of work from political life and professions from civic culture.... Public work highlights the productive, world-building aspects of politics, the need to solve public problems by bridging different interests and perspectives. It also suggests a generative understanding of power, not only power *over* the dominant view, but power *to*, power that comes from creating public relationships, tapping new talent and imagination, and creating democratic cultures.

This brings into view a different concept of the role of professionals, shifting from a service-delivery model to catalytic and organizing roles....

These traditions became translated into the contemporary world in a myriad of ways. As the nation industrialized, civic populist intellectuals, such as Jane Addams, Liberty Hyde Bailey, James Weldon Johnson, Zora Neale Hurston, and others, played important roles in translating older ideas of productive labors to the new society by emphasizing the training of professionals for catalytic, energizing public work....

The challenge today is to revive the organizing skills, the professional sensibilities, and the larger strategic framework of the 1930s and their continuing legacy in SCLC and broad-based community organizing. We also need to adapt these for a radically different age....

... An organizing approach in higher education is different than approaches to change based on dissemination of information, service delivery, or moralized protest. It engages people through their diverse interests, builds alliances that take account of power relationships and institutional cultures, and has a strong, relational approach....

Technocracy, the expert stance outside a common life, seeking to manipulate the world, sustains academic practices as well as professions as self-referential, abstract, and full of techniques, devoid of public life.... Democratic society, rather than democratic state, entails a fundamentally different conception of the academic and intellectual's role, a shift from critic and outsider to engaged intellectual who helps generate constructive action.... Our broadest challenge of higher education is to advance democratic values and to join in movements to build citizen-centered democratic societies. This is the only real way to bring professionals, who see themselves often as outsiders, back into a common civic life. It is also how, together, we will develop the civic power to guide a world spinning out of control.

In the effort to redefine scholarship as a democratic practice, the extension programs of land-grant universities are potentially key intervention points. However, typical of higher education as a whole, the dominant understanding of the land-grant mission, with its language of "service" and "outreach," is based on a conventional technical view of expertise that can be disabling to citizen self-rule. In this essay from *Agent of Democracy*, Scott Peters, Associate Professor in the Department of Education at Cornell University, argues for scholarship that is interactive and political rather than detached and technical and provides concrete examples of public scholarship in action.

FOR MORE THAN A CENTURY, many scholars in land-grant colleges of agriculture and human ecology . . . have established one of the most important democratic traditions of public scholarship in American higher education. . . .

It has been and continues to be obscured by the prevailing view of the land-grant mission as responsive, narrowly instrumental, and apolitical public service. Also, it has been and continues to be marginalized by technocratic tendencies and forces, and by the research university norm of civic detachment. Additionally, the story I tell illuminates the conflicting and conflicted nature of scholars' views about their political roles and stances, including how they should understand and work through what historian Thomas Bender has referred to as "the dilemma of the relation of expertise and democracy."

The national land-grant system was established through the Morrill Acts of 1862 and 1890 and the Equity in Education Land-Grant Status Act of 1994. It consists of 105 institutions located in all 50 states and several U.S. territories. A unique structural feature of this system is its institutionalization in colleges of agriculture and human ecology of permanent mechanisms for engaging faculty, staff, and students as active participants in the world beyond the campus....

...The prevailing view in academic literatures, official institutional rhetoric, and informal culture characterizes the land-grant mission (in both historical and contemporary contexts) as "public service." It positions the land-grant system as the historical exemplar of the so-called "service ideal" in American higher education....

... There are four main problems with the prevailing view of the historical nature and significance of the land-grant mission:

- First, *it is entirely responsive and one-directional*. It characterizes the land-grant system's engagement with the world beyond the campus as consisting only of one-way transfers and applications of technical knowledge and expertise that are made in response to the demands for help by external clients and constituencies.

- Second, *it is too narrow and instrumental*. It casts the history of the land-grant system's public purposes and work as being about only technical, material, and economic matters.

- Third, *it is embarrassingly self-congratulatory*. It implies that the history of the pursuit of the land-grant mission is one of complete, continuous, and unambiguous success.

- Finally—and for me, most important—*it is apolitical*. Instead of using a political language of public relationships and work involving people with different types and levels of interests, knowledge, expertise, and power, the prevailing view employs a mechanical language of responsive public service that focuses on the provision of technical solutions to technical problems through instrumental transactions between active and allegedly "unbiased" experts and passive, needy clients. Such a language obscures the politics of scholars' engagement in the world beyond the campus. It also reinforces the self-congratulatory story line about land-grant history....

Contrary to the prevailing view of the historical nature and significance of the land-grant mission, the public purposes and work of many scholars who were employed by land-grant colleges of agriculture during the late 19th and early 20th centuries were not limited to responsive technical problem solving. They also included the proactive pursuit of what Liberty Hyde Bailey referred to in 1897 as a "self-sustaining" agriculture.... Bailey viewed the pursuit of a self-sustaining agriculture as a multidimensional project that had technical, scientific, moral, cultural, political, and even spiritual dimensions. In his view, such a project would both require and result in the development of a new rural civilization "worthy of the best American ideals."...

In both the individual and focus group interviews we have conducted, faculty told more than 75 practice stories.... In these stories, faculty spoke of why and how they developed close, working relationships with particular individuals, groups, and organizations, including small- and large-scale farmers and their associations, ... golf course managers, government agencies, legislators and elected officials, nongovernment organizations (NGOs), and community organizations and institutions.

Most of the practice stories faculty members told focus on social problems related to the environment. These include environmental pollution and human health problems caused (or thought to be caused) by farming practices, or by the use of chemicals to control weeds and pests.... Some stories focus on work related to public policy debates, such as whether genetically modified organisms (GMOs) should be promoted, adopted, regulated, or banned.... Other stories involve ... migrant labor, racial, ethnic, and class issues, zoning and land-use planning, urban sprawl, ... poverty, economic decline, population loss, the loss of a sense of community, youth violence and substance abuse, and ... student achievement in rural and small-town schools.

Consider the following view of the land-grant mission that was articulated by a professor in the natural science discipline of plant breeding:

> I would argue that the mission of the land-grant is interaction with the people in the state. If we want to contribute to the collective wisdom—and that includes us as everyone else around the state— then I think it means interacting with people.... What can we do

> to contribute to greater understanding or better dialogue or public
> policy that really will help address them? ... That's what I think of
> as the land-grant mission for our college....

This view positions land-grant faculty as proactive participants in public work: not as volunteers, but as scholars. It both compels and authorizes scholars to establish reciprocal relationships between the university and the public that hold both democratic and academic promise. At their best, such relationships are not only civic or political in nature, in the sense that they involve deliberation and action about public issues. They are also scholarly, in the sense that they serve as a crucial means of informing, shaping, and sometimes even conducting a scholar's research.

But [a professor in a natural science discipline] add[ed] the following: "This view of the land-grant mission is a minority view in my department. The majority view is that we're here to advance knowledge." ... What we should learn from this is that scholars who hold highly interactive views of the land-grant mission are not only up against the prevailing apolitical public service view of that mission, but also the research university norm of civic detachment. When these are combined, as I think they often are, it places public scholars in an exceedingly difficult position....

In an important essay published in 1996, Eugene Rice spoke of the need to make a place for the "new American scholar." According to Rice, one of the defining characteristics of the new American scholar is deep engagement in rather than detachment from civic life. Ironically, in land-grant colleges the present challenge is to keep a place for a class of *old* American scholars, a class that has long embraced and enacted—however imperfectly—the pledge civic professionals make to "deploy their technical expertise and judgment not only skillfully but for public-regarding ends and in a public-regarding way."

Across a range of fields, from health care to journalism, organizations have powerful incentives to reinforce a clear distinction between experts and citizens, even when they intend to fulfill public responsibilities. In this context, Albert W. Dzur, Associate Professor of Political Science at Bowling Green State University, reflects on the politics of public scholarship in an interview conducted by David Brown. According to Dzur, public scholarship is part of a larger movement toward "democratic professionalism," which sees collaboration with citizens as central to fulfilling professional and institutional responsibilities.

Brown: As I understand your term, *democratic professionalism*, it is when professionals "share authority" with members of the public "over tasks that affect them." Such professionals serve as "facilitators." Your studies focus on hospitals, clinics, newspapers, courtrooms, and correctional facilities. Where else is democratic professionalism asserting itself?

Dzur: I regularly work with graduate students in public administration and have noticed an increasing appreciation for the idea that they might become democratic professionals. They see the public as a somewhat chaotic force in the life of an administrator: the public can be ignorant about trade-offs that have to be made because of tight budgets, can be oblivious to the rules and regulations that constrain official action, and yet the public is, ultimately, "the boss," and, on good days, the reason one gets up in the morning to begin a new workday.

Additionally, they realize that conventional methods of communicating with their constituents are defunct: surveys, town-hall meetings, ad hoc forums held to assuage fears are incapable of fostering meaningful two-way dialogue. Like the recent interest in the concept of public deliberation among public administration scholars, I think the idea of professionals collaborating with lay people in ongoing departmental decision making, in sponsoring community review boards and similar forums, has appeal for a new generation of practitioners. Speaking more generally, democratic professionalism aligns well with their preference for horizontal rather than vertical organizations.

Brown: Do you see more faculty members becoming attracted to such professionalism?

Dzur: We have begun to see a drift towards a more democratic understanding of professionalism among academics. Harry Boyte and others have discovered a deep dissatisfaction among even the most successful academics about their work and culture, a felt loss of agency. On one side are trustees and presidents and provosts demanding more accountability to the public in the forms of teaching for real-world skills and grant-funded research. On the other side are social capitalists demanding a different kind of public accountability through more service learning and scholarship of engagement. Both forms of public pressure are experienced as confining to many faculty, especially when applied crudely in the process of promotion and tenure. Democratic professionalism offers an alternative understanding of public accountability more congruent with traditional conceptions of the university as a cooperative community of knowledge seekers. Collaborating with lay people and allowing professional practices to be open to critical reflection from outsiders—a kind of "in-reach," as opposed to conventional academic outreach programming—are ways of narrowing the social distance between campuses and the wider communities they depend upon for students and for funding.

Brown: If "local knowledge" is important, why are many professionals ignorant of its importance or resistant to seeking it out? Do you think this is primarily driven by economic self-interest? That is, professionals have to make a living so why include those without their training and credentials?

Dzur: Your question is about the interests that keep professionals at arm's length from lay people. Sociologists of the professions describe a highly competitive jockeying for position between overlapping occupations: paralegals vs. lawyers, EMTs vs. MDs vs. RNs, psychiatrists vs. psychologists. An image of commanding competence in a specialized technique and body of knowledge is important in distinguishing your trade and this explains why professionals frequently obfuscate similarities and exaggerate differences from everyday knowledge. A first-year law student once told me that he wanted to be a lawyer because he liked the idea of wearing a suit to work. Seemingly superficial, to be sure, but it speaks to a deep need we have to be respected, be distinguished in some way.

Some of the most competent professionals I have encountered, however, are also the most open to local knowledge. Like Socrates, they understand the limits of their knowledge, how circumscribed their awareness is, and, in fact, how the skills and techniques they learned in graduate and professional school can sometimes hinder as well as help. Knowing their limits plus having confidence in themselves leads to the willingness to share responsibility for a task with a lay person.

The relationship between professional and local knowledge is complicated. In the book,[15] I talk about the importance of both collaboration and contestation, meaning that there is solid middle ground for professionals to occupy between being dismissive and being deferential to lay people. Democratic professionals welcome and encourage intermediary spaces—real, concrete places for regular meetings—where those with professional and those with local knowledge can test, learn from, and also dispute each other.

Brown: Please say more about, what you call, "the intermediary realm" where professionals "possess the power to distract, encourage, limit, and inform democratic deliberation."

Dzur: As an example of something that exists in this intermediary realm, consider the ethics committees mandated for hospitals and clinics as part of

---

[15] Albert W. Dzur, *Democratic Professionalism: Citizen Participation and the Reconstruction of Professional Ethics, Identity, and Practice* (University Park: Pennsylvania State University Press, 2008).

their accreditation process. These reflect the general interest organizations have for dialogue, communication, transparency, and a sharing of responsibility for difficult decisions. One explicit goal for these committees is to educate hospital staff and the broader community on norms of humane health care that recognize patients as full-fledged participants in their own treatment even while they are in an organization that moves at an extremely rapid pace and follows complex rules. Such committees have the potential to be public forums—open spaces for reflective moral dialogue that will foster community conversations about tricky issues, such as organ donation, genetic testing, and physician-assisted suicide. Unfortunately, they are typically dominated by insiders and regulars from the medical staff who have particular interests in shielding their organization's practices from critical scrutiny. I serve on one of these committees and was struck recently by a story a senior staff member told about an area hospital that prided itself on having only one documented medical mistake and that it had been quickly corrected without any harm to the patient. Either that was the best hospital on Earth, or, more likely, it was one where medical mistakes were defined extremely narrowly, not reported, not investigated, or some combination of these factors. So professionals can encourage the kind of free-wheeling, open, and brutally honest public dialogue their organizations need to root out problems and serve people better, or they can do what is more comfortable—but much less useful to their organization in the long run.

Brown: What are some of the social problems that are amenable to the practice of democratic professionalism?

Dzur: Each of the cases of democratic professionalism I write about in the book connect up to social problems policy people call "wicked" because they are immune to simple solutions. The criminal justice system, the medical establishment, and the news business are all in crisis and nobody knows this better than practitioners themselves. They realize that improving their relationship with the public is critical to breaking out of wicked cycles that are ruining their profession and gaining them little ground. One out of every hundred American adults are in jail or prison as a result of "get tough" policies that criminal justice professionals know are short-sighted, if only because the public really does not want to fund more prison construction. Affordable and accessible health care eludes us even as doctors spend less time with more patients for less compensation. Political journalism has turned to infotainment because that sells, but it is has also contributed to an increasingly cynical culture that doesn't ultimately want to buy anything the so-called mainstream media (MSM) has to sell. By bringing lay people into professional domains, familiarizing them with some of the imperfections and gray areas in decision making by sharing tasks, the reformers I am interested in create public relationships that are needed to begin to work through these wicked problems.

Brown: John Dewey claimed the public's "most urgent problem" is "to find and identify itself." Do democratic professionals think this to be important?

Dzur: Democratic professionals realize that helping publics find themselves is an urgent problem for both citizens and professionals. Organizations as different as hospitals, institutions of criminal justice, universities have similar self-images: at some level they serve the public. But how to understand this relationship between professionals in complex organizations and the people who are served? On one traditional account, the profession serves the public on its own terms: the court professionals know what justice is, the medical professionals know what health is, the journalists know what news is. Professionals are "social trustees" who earn a significant degree of work autonomy and independence in the establishment of performance standards by contributing their specialized skills and knowledge for the good of the larger society. But they also play a dominant role in defining what that good is.

Since the 1960s, public opinion regarding many professions has been increasingly skeptical as the social trustee image of doctors, lawyers, academics, and others has been tarnished by what appears to be a rise in self-seeking behavior on the part of practitioners. College administrators, for example, feeling the pressure of governing boards who share the public's skepticism, have responded with market-oriented demands for real-world skills and job training for graduates. But a market-oriented professionalism, though it may seem to those outside the organization as an improvement over self-satisfied social trustee attitudes, is repellant to many practitioners who sacrificed time and energy to specialized study or apprenticeship and who are passionate about their work not because it sells but because it has meaning and significance. Academic professionals cultivate critical thinking that reveals hard truths about society, they preserve old ideas, old images, old sounds, and they investigate the natural world not to produce tangible and marketable goods or services, but to create a better public life nonetheless.

Brown: And so democratic professionals are a different breed?

Dzur: Democratic professionalism is a mode of steering organizations towards the long-term and open-ended interests of the public that is responsive to contributions of both professionals and lay people. It is a new way of expressing a very old idea, or, put differently, an attempt at naming some practices we hardly even notice because we take them for granted. Consider the jury trial, for example. Jurors literally cocreate justice with court professionals by testing evidence, legal theories, and ultimately even the law of the land against everyday knowledge, practical experience, and wide-ranging moral awareness. Juries check the power of court professionals, but they also, as Tocqueville noticed long ago, increase the legitimacy of courts and therefore reinforce professional authority even as they share in the collaborative task of judgment.

So that wonderful comment of Dewey's from *The Public and Its Problems* is precisely on target. Democratic professionals recognize that healthy organizations, institutions, practices require active collaboration with real, not symbolic or imagined, publics. These publics help the professions find themselves.

Brown: Finally, could it be said that democratic professionalism is a different kind of "politics"?

Dzur: Max Weber closed his *Protestant Ethic* with the chilling description of the "specialists without spirit, sensualists without heart" trapped within the "iron cage of modernity." Democratic professionalism gives voice to reformers who recognize the vulnerability of complex organizations dominated by experts and managers who follow rational strategies and formal rules but have lost contact with the living values of an ongoing community, what Weber called "substantive rationality." A reformer I interviewed about why citizen participation was important to the restorative justice program he had helped plan said he wanted to "build imperfection into the system." He meant that the administration of justice needs citizens on the inside of the organization to adequately do its job of fair and humane public safety. Even more strikingly, he meant by "imperfection" that he wanted citizens to play a serious role in his organization without turning into professionals themselves, repeat players jaundiced by seeing and judging what they think they have seen and judged a thousand times before. Citizen participation in his organization was a circulatory system that kept it alive to social reality. Justice, health and well-being, public information, education, these are objectives that modernity has delivered to complex organizations staffed by experts and professionals, headed up by managers, but they are inadequate to the tasks and have always been so because these objectives are only given meaning in ongoing concrete social interactions and relationships.

The answer to your question is "yes," this is a different kind of politics: participatory, responsible, collaborative. Democratic professionals share institutional power, share tasks and responsibility, and share experiences with lay citizens all in the hope of breaking free of the iron cage that separates modern organizations from the communities that give them purpose and meaning. University faculty, for example, can no longer rest on the laurels of a received professionalism but must reframe what it means to be an academic by more fully incorporating the public—not just fee-paying students and parents, and not just trustees—into bearing responsibility for ongoing communities of learning and scholarship. This is a politics of imperfection and will be messy, time-consuming, and open-ended; everything democratic, everything with heart and spirit always is!

CHAPTER FOUR

Universities and Communities: The Politics of Democratic Relationships

ONE OF THE CORE PROBLEMS in democracy is the relationship between citizen-centered politics and strong community networks.[16] Community networks play a key role by providing the spaces in which citizens associate together to learn the habits and skills of democratic self-rule. A primary factor in the flourishing of communities may be the extent to which such networks are self-organizing, based on the energy, skills, and resources of the community, rather than those of experts, external organizations, and bureaucratic institutions.

---

[16] For example, see Vaughn L. Grisham Jr., *Tupelo: The Evolution of a Community* (Dayton, OH: Kettering Foundation Press, 1999).

Self-organizing community networks are more likely to lead to sustainable and effective organic politics.

As institutions with enormous technical expertise and economic resources, colleges and universities in particular are powerful actors with the ability to either facilitate or discourage the development of community networks in their towns and neighborhoods. Campuses around the country advertise their collaborations with communities, and their mission statements refer to values of equality and reciprocity in these relationships. Too often, however, these programs reflect a larger pattern of politics as usual, with conventional power relations and citizens treated as passive and deficient clients in need of help from above, and civic engagement defined in terms dictated by institutional interests.[17] At the same time, a different kind of politics is beginning to emerge, in which universities partner with community organizations to build their capacities for self-organizing civic change and end cycles of dysfunction and dependency.

---

[17] John A. Creighton and Richard C. Harwood, "The Organization-First Approach: How Intermediary Organizations Approach Civic Engagement and Communities" (Bethesda, MD: The Harwood Institute, 2007).

Changing power dynamics goes against the grain of institutional self-interest, and universities tend to define civic engagement in their own terms. Unfortunately, as a result, the voices of community partners are too often missing from conventional discussions of the relationship between universities and communities. In a recent issue of *HEX*, Sean Creighton, Executive Director of the Southwestern Ohio Council for Higher Education, explores the reasons for the dysfunctional relationships between higher education institutions and community partners. He argues that listening to community partners is the key to sustainable programs with democratic power dynamics.

I WAS NEAR THE FINAL STAGES of my doctoral program, determined to produce research that would make a meaningful contribution to the field of civic engagement in higher education....

A group of students was developing a shared vision for local neighborhoods as part of a community-building project. During a public presentation of the shared vision, a community member stood and thanked the students for their work and commitment to strengthening the neighborhoods. He then asked, "What now? You've worked with us to develop the shared vision —how will you stay involved?" The students replied that the semester was over and, essentially, their work was done. In that moment, I understood that the students did not realize the expectations community members had for sustained engagement. I had found my dissertation research question: *What do community organizations look for (and expect) in a successful civic engagement partnership with higher education institutions?...*

... The research design and process sought to understand the expectations, needs, desires, and perceptions of community organizations that had partnered with several colleges and universities in the Greater Dayton region of Ohio.... The participants developed 10 community-partner indicators of engagement to be used in negotiating and assessing their campus-community partnerships (download the complete Community Partner Indicators of Engagement at www.soche.org/councils/scholarship.asp)....

For each indicator, the participants developed associated effective and ineffective descriptors.... While service learning was revered in the literature and was becoming a commonly adopted pedagogy, the participants in the study exposed a different perspective on service learning. While they supported its impact on student learning and development, they also perceived serious issues and "felt used by service-learning programs." One participant from a small nonprofit that serves teenagers drew nods from the others when she said:

> Yesterday when I got back to the office ... one of my staff came in and said they got 16 calls from interns—students from University B. It was a class of social workers. They came to class and were given a list of agencies to call for a 32-hour placement.... My assistant called the professor and said, "Stop it." ... That's just rude and lazy on the part of the faculty. There's no preparation for the students or advanced discussion with the agencies. While we want to assist, we cannot do 32-hour placements.... We need to do police background checks on anyone that works in our programs.

... Yet another participant from a social service agency identified student entitlement as a common problem, adding:

> The students, especially the undergraduate students, come in and they have this entitlement.... And I know this from my own children, who are very successful, but they do have this certain entitlement mentality and, for better or for worse, whatever the generation is called, I think that's part of it....

During the study, the participants discussed in detail their feelings about relationships with local colleges and universities and, in particular, faculty. Participants felt "disrespected" by higher education partners, expressing the opinion that higher education had an "elitist attitude."... Consequently, they saw the remedy being a process that engages campuses and their community partners in discussions that alleviate feelings of mistrust, disrespect, and inferiority....

The participants commented frequently that the long-term effective-ness of campus-community engagement would be significantly enhanced if higher education approached partnerships from a standpoint of equal-ity. Unfortunately, they felt "ignored" by higher education, noting, "there has to be fair acknowledgement of the value of each partner." Participants expressed their sincere gratitude toward campuses that included them in the entire process. For the participants, a productive process provides the opportunity to dialogue with peers, reflect on the meaning of effective campus-community partnerships, and agree on action steps that improve campus-community relationships.... Once everybody understands the ground rules, you write them down." One participant suggested creating a manifesto:

> We need a manifesto—a bill of rights; something that says we have come together, we have looked at partnerships, what we expect, and here it is. Now, we want you to be a partner, we want you to play, but we've got to be on equal footing or it does not equal a partnership. We want to make the partnership real, and it is not real now....

... Knowing that community organizations are vital local assets that have existed, in some cases, for as long as many of our nation's colleges and universities, it is, therefore, important to continue to advocate for a deeper understanding of community partners. If higher education seeks to make long-lasting, valuable contributions in their communities, then campus leaders must listen closely to their community partners. Kent Keith, editor of *The Responsive University: Restructuring for Higher Performance*, wrote in the conclusion, "it is when the activities of our colleges and universities are aligned with the highest-priority needs of society that we will have the greatest positive impact." Such an alignment comes from a place of com-plete engagement. One of the community participants in this study similarly commented, "You've got to have, I think, some sort of commonality in your mission, or at least be complementary in your mission, for your partnership to be given a chance to succeed." This notion is illustrated by the indicator of mission compatibility, which states that an effective partnership "flourishes because of compatibility of missions, creating a meaningful and complemen-tary intersect."

One of the most difficult obstacles to genuinely democratic relationships between universities and community partners is the powerful institutional incentives for universities to promote their own interests. The most innovative programs we have seen have put serious thought into creating new organizational structures that do not rely upon the conventional model of ownership by a single institution. In *Voices of Hope*, Nan Kari and Nan Skelton, cofounders of the Jane Addams School (JAS), tell the story of the founding of a partnership that provides collaborative education in democratic citizenship to college students and local immigrant groups. JAS currently involves students from 11 colleges and universities, with the Center for Democracy and Citizenship at the University of Minnesota as the main supporting institution. The organizational structure they describe is unique, but the story has implications for anyone thinking seriously about relationships between universities and communities.

THE ROOTS of the Jane Addams School for Democracy grew from the life experiences, values, and public passions of those who came together in 1996 with a vision to create a democratic organization and egalitarian way of working and learning across cultures. The democratic traditions of progressive 20th-century leaders like Jane Addams, Ella Baker, Myles Horton, and John Dewey inspire our work. From the beginning, we intended that JAS would address large questions about education and democracy....

A passion for serious educational reform animated early conversations and writing by students and other founders. An early analysis found in the JAS archival papers, describes the contemporary education crisis in this way:

> Students' own lives, cultures, and backgrounds are rarely seen as learning resources.... Educational institutions are disconnected from the places in which they are located. Conversely, surrounding communities are rarely seen as rich with cultures and settings that provide opportunities for learning.... There are few opportunities for students to reflect deeply on the moral implications of what they are learning.... There is an unmet need in our educational system to engage young people in work of public importance.

We started with the assumption that U.S.-born young people together with immigrant families could cultivate civic identities and learn democratic skills through involvement in serious public work. Building the Jane Addams School was and continues to be a public work to which many have contributed. It has provided us the context to better understand concepts and practices of democratic education....

On the evening of September 23, 1996, we launched JAS anticipating that we would open the door and see what happened. With reciprocity as the guiding principle, we trusted people would teach us what they wanted to learn, and we would do likewise. Crowded into a small room in the Neighborhood House settlement on the West Side of St. Paul, a handful of college students, a few faculty, 12 Hmong people (mostly women), along with several native Spanish speakers, began to craft what and how people wanted to learn together. We developed a format using a learning-circle method adapted from the Highlander model. Each learning circle held a 30-minute "cultural exchange," carried on in three languages, followed by self-directed study in learning pairs....

Ten years later, more than 1500 participants at JAS—Hmong, East Africans, and Latin Americans—have become citizens....

JAS began with three supporting institutions in the Twin Cities: Neighborhood House, the College of St. Catherine, and the University of

Minnesota (particularly, the Center for Democracy and Citizenship...). The evolution of these relationships yields lessons about places for experimentation connected with, but not governed or owned by, any one institution. For instance, the faculty at the College of St. Catherine had redesigned the core curriculum and wanted to experiment with a more active, student-centered pedagogy. Frustrated by the structures that organize and constrain reform in higher education, faculty and student leaders sought opportunities free of these structures to develop practices in active learning. JAS provided an alternative learning environment for students and faculty. Likewise Neighborhood House leaders wanted an opportunity to experiment with the recovery and potential adaptation of earlier, more democratic practices of settlement work to their current model. In these ways, the supporting institutions could invest resources and energy in the enterprise, observe what could happen with alternative structures, claim and implement its innovations, and, we hoped, reform the institution from the margins. There is some evidence that this is happening. For instance, the University of Minnesota launched a civic mission initiative with the broad purpose of rebuilding its institutional civic culture and land-grant tradition. One facet of that work seeks to identify and understand the dynamics of reciprocal community relationships in addressing public problems. The university names its partnership with JAS as one successful model of institutional civic engagement and effective community-based learning for students.

JAS is not a 501(c)(3) organization; it exists within the "parentheses" of a network of supporting organizations that relate more directly to JAS than they do to each other. This structure proved an effective way for JAS to maintain accountability to the community, to foundations, and to its collaborating institutions, while ensuring creativity and shared ownership. The arrangement provides greater flexibility for fiscal administration while allowing JAS to link into existing institutional infrastructure like budget systems, human resources, and technology, without having to carry the full cost of developing and maintaining its own infrastructure....

The rise of expert knowledge and the socialization of the professional class has shaped public problem solving in profound and complicated ways. The default tendency to assign authority to professional expertise reflects an unequal power dynamic, which creates a stranglehold around citizen imagination and creativity. This dynamic poses an enormous barrier, ironically at a time when many immigrants have the energy and the inclination to contribute to the community.... Engaging in public work has been the vehicle for people to see individual and collective talents in a new light, and in the process, challenge cultural assumptions about who can lead....

... Relationships between JAS and institutions of higher education develop over time and with different levels of intensity. Typically colleges and community organizations form partnerships with a specific task in mind, often to seek funds.... Impressive publications showcase the partnership and its outcomes. Though productive, these partnerships are often one-dimensional, particularly when the responsibility for building and sustaining the relationship falls to a few designated people—someone on campus and a "partner" in a community nonprofit. In contrast, JAS builds relationship with colleges "brick by brick" in multidimensional ways and with many people involved: through shared research, curriculum development, faculty development, student work-study, and internships. In its largest framing, we describe the JAS-college affiliation in terms of shared public work to build civic skills so that diverse people can cocreate a better common life.

With a mission to assist the development of local communities, the land-grant university extension system has great potential to model democratic partnerships between higher education institutions and communities. Although the dominant approach continues to be top-down dissemination and technical assistance, political development was the central aim of David Pelletier, Associate Professor of Nutritional Sciences at Cornell University, in building the North Country Community Food and Economic Security Network through a series of search conferences with farmers, consumers, retailers, and residents in upstate New York. This profile of Pelletier, based on an interview conducted by Margot Hittleman and Scott Peters, documents his struggle to redefine the university as a public institution that, rather than reinforcing cycles of dependency on expertise, enables communities to become self-organizing civic agents.

THE NORTH COUNTRY PROJECT began in 1996. The area is very rural, sparsely populated, and very poor. The poverty statistics are as bad as they are in New York City. The area is very badly affected by the decline of the dairy industry and the regional economy in general.

Community food security is a concept that's being pushed by the Community Food Security Coalition, a national organization. It has two aspects. One is access to safe, nutritious food by low-income people. That's the traditional aspect. The other is concern with the structure of the food system and the desire to relocalize as many functions or activities as possible in the food system, because of concern about corporate control and environmental impacts. I also wanted to test the meaning and importance of the official concept of community food security as articulated by the Community Food Security Coalition—test it with real people and real communities. Was it just a bunch of "yuppie" food activists who were pushing it because it was meaningful to them? I purposely wanted people in the North Country to play with this concept and find meaning in it themselves and label it for themselves. The Community Food Security Coalition was saying there are problems with the mainstream food system and here are some alternatives. And those alternatives revolve around relocalization. And there's a whole set of values underlying that: environmental, social justice, anticorporate, all the rest. I could see some virtue in those alternative values, but I wondered how meaningful they were to people on the ground.

Rather than doing an opinion poll or launching some questionnaire-based approach, I thought the only way to answer that question was through action, through deliberation and action. And so, in a way, the project was one large attempt to give people an opportunity to reflect on their food system and come up with action plans that better reflected their values and aspirations. And then help them to organize to fulfill those visions to the extent they deem desirable within the resources they have.

The basic sequence of the search conference begins with creating a shared history during the first session. The next session you do the ideal future, which answers the question, if we could have our ideal future, what would it look like? Then you move on to the probable future: if we take no action, what will the future look like? That creates the contrast that makes the choice to take action obvious. From that point on, you start moving into the more traditional components of strategic planning, saying, "How can we convert the present into this ideal future?" You break the suggestions into elements, and then you develop tasks and goals around each element. People organize into work groups to deal with the tasks and goals.

In terms of follow-up work after the search conferences, we went back with a post-search conference event in each county to bring people back together. Even though right after the event they had all said, "Yes, yes. We want to get back together," typically only about a third to a half would come back together. At the end, I very explicitly reminded them: "We're on call.

If you need something, let us know. Maybe we can help. But from here on out, you're in the driver's seat. What you get out of this will depend on how much you put into it." [In an earlier project in other communities] we felt as though we were grabbing them by the hand and pulling them along, instead of playing the supportive role. As soon as we stopped coming, they stopped meeting. We felt that, in an ironic way, the external assistance at some point began to erode the development of a sense of ownership and responsibility for moving forward on their own. So [in the North Country Project] we used the phrase, "on tap, not on top" numerous times. That's the philosophy that we were playing out.

After the search conference, either the extension people, the community-action people, or somebody in the community had to display leadership and support some or all of those working groups. In one county, for instance, the extension educator, who was an ag educator who had been involved from the beginning, tried to do that. He convened the groups. He helped move them through their meetings. He set up a newsletter. Then his new executive director came in and quickly told him, "Get back to what you're supposed to be doing. What are you doing with these groups? I don't want you spending time on that." The director wanted him to spend his time on the financial management of dairy farms, which included helping them with their tax returns. Very traditional stuff. That guy ended up quitting extension.

About a year later, this executive director became one of the biggest sup-porters of community food security. They ended up hiring a crackerjack community organizer, a Hispanic woman who's still doing unbelievable stuff up there.

The mission of the land-grant system is fundamentally about being a public institution. As such, I think we should be doing work that the private sector does not have the incentive to do or addressing issues that might be created in part by the private sector (corporate as well as societal). When problems arise, public institutions are responsible for addressing them in some fashion. I'm a strong believer in the university's three-fold mission of research, education, and extension, although I certainly don't see extension in the dissemination role. I think we should be involved in more communi-ty development approaches. We should be facilitators of a development in social improvement.

In this exchange, Marguerite (Peggy) Shaffer, Associate Professor of American Studies at Miami University, reflects with David Brown on the challenges facing the effort to create a "public culture" through relationships between universities and communities. As Shaffer observes, these relationships develop within a privatized culture that emphasizes discrete projects and individual acts of volunteerism. Shaffer describes her experience in creating the Act Locally program, which shifts the focus to building relationships and strengthening civic capacities.

Brown: The last time we talked together you saw "the public as a process." What do you think is needed to get that process started and sustained?

Shaffer: Revitalizing public agency, public work, and public engagement is going to require widespread culture change. Over the past 30 years, the dominant political culture has successfully substituted a privatized ideal of the free market for an engaged and democratic civil society. In the process, the capacity of individuals to think beyond themselves and their own individual rights and privatized desires has been diminished, if not incapacitated. As William Galston has argued, the market has become the defining metaphor of our time; so much so that I think it is sometimes difficult for us to imagine ourselves in anything other than therapeutic terms and to act as anything more than consumers and spectators. In other words, over the past half-century we have become increasingly privatized individuals. We might exist in civil society and function within it, but we do so within an individualized frame of reference for all our actions.

We need to relearn how to think and act in public terms; we need to rebuild our capacity for public engagement; we need to systematically reeducate ourselves in the skills and competencies necessary for public agency and public work. Ideally this would mean reinvigorating the deliberative democratic process, prioritizing the needs of sustaining local communities, and reasserting the role of universities and colleges as public institutions. Given the current state of our political process, the status of our economy, and the global environmental crisis, this seems like a daunting task; especially when you consider the scholarship that suggests that in times of scarcity and crisis people turn inward toward self-preservation and economic security. But when I ask myself what I can do as a scholar and teacher and when I look out at the desire my students have to make a better future, I see opportunities to reconnect higher education to its public mission. I think there is real potential for educational institutions to instigate this kind of culture change.

To me the purpose of education is not only about being able to think and act beyond the self, it is about understanding and embracing the necessity for thinking and acting beyond the self. And to me this is what democracy is all about. My work on public culture is my way of reaffirming and making explicit the inherent connections between democracy and education.

Brown: Sean Creighton reports that some communities feel "used" by service-learning programs. Creighton also noted that a sense of "student entitlement" is resented, and that communities sometimes are seen as "laboratories," which produces "ineffective" partnerships. Have you found such impressions to be a problem in your work, and, if so, how do you deal with them?

Shaffer: Creighton is right on the mark. The problem he identifies—"student entitlement" and community exploitation reflects the way in which colleges and universities have forgotten their public mission and separated themselves from the communities that support them. In our multiyear community-based Acting Locally Think Tank, students often come into the program with an agenda: they have been told throughout high school that service is an excellent way to build their résumés; they come with particular objectives and projects in mind; they have been socialized by an educational culture that equates abstract or theoretical knowledge with expertise. This, combined with the idealism and naiveté of their age and the current weak status of public culture, makes it very difficult for them to see beyond their own goals and objectives and to acknowledge their limited experience and perspective. They have also been socialized by an educational system that puts incredible pressure on them to see their college experience in terms of preprofessional training rather than as an opportunity to experiment with new ideas, to learn new things, to broaden their minds, to advance their education, and to learn the skills and responsibilities necessary to sustain a functional democratic society.

I think we as educators reinforce these inclinations through the culture of expertise and professionalism that has come to dominate higher education. By defining knowledge creation and dissemination in terms of disciplinary expertise, we legitimate the idea that we are preparing students as experts with a specialized kind of knowledge that they can then impart to ignorant and passive community members. Faculty are part of the problem as well, because as scholarly knowledge generation and dissemination has become more insular and professionalized, faculty have become part of this culture of expertise. From this perspective, the skills and knowledge of community members, with long-term commitment to publics and to their communities, and their extensive experience in public problem solving are either invisible or not valued because of the lack of professional training or disciplinary expertise. Community members who have been engaged in solving public problems and creating sustainable communities as part of their everyday experience and practice as citizens and community members are seen as passive clients.

Brown: How then does the Acting Locally program deal with, as you call it, "the culture of expertise and professionalism"?

Shaffer: With the Acting Locally program, we have sought to counteract this sense of superiority and entitlement while supporting our community partners by shifting the organizing focus and attention away from projects and focusing on creating and sustaining trusting partnerships with communities. I make it a point to respond to student questions about projects and outcomes by asking students about community needs and how they plan to build and sustain lasting partnerships with community members. After students have examined the larger theory and history of globalization and learned about the history and current issues that are affecting the communities they will be working in, we have them engage in one-on-ones with community members, encouraging them to make individual connections with a range of individuals who are committed to creating sustainable communities. We introduce them to community asset mapping to teach them to see communities as complex and dynamic public organisms where diverse individuals with a range of experiences, skills, and interests work together in an ongoing process. Our goal is to shift the frame away from cataloging community problems and weaknesses and toward an understanding of how people in communities come together even if only provisionally to define and shape the places in which they live and work. We want students to be clear about the skills they have—time, energy, enthusiasm, research capacity, information-gathering skills—and how they might share these skills with community partners over the long-term and learn from them to gain a better sense of public agency. The faculty involved in this project worked to articulate how we might systematically redefine our liberal education principles (thinking critically, understanding context, engaging other learners, reflecting, and acting) in distinctly public terms. As a consequence of this work, we have tried to make a conscious shift away from problem solving to partnership building.

Our success will be measured by how well we can sustain the trusting relationships we have developed and whether we can institutionalize the community partnerships we have forged. But I know in the long term, the only way we can begin to make serious inroads against this condescending mind-set and the divide between universities and communities is to breathe new life and real meaning and commitment into our public mission at Miami. It means making a real commitment to creating sustainable communities, sharing resources and knowledge, providing a space for public debate and discussion, prioritizing the generation and dissemination of actionable knowledge, and privileging public agency and public work as the most important skills students will gain through their college education.

Brown: Commenting on the Creighton study of campus-community partnerships, David Mathews regretted that too many ignore building civic capacity. What do you think accounts for this failure?

Shaffer: I think this failure to build civic capacity reflects the failure of institutions of higher education to fulfill their public missions. Although colleges and universities claim and assert their value as public institutions, they no longer prioritize or organize themselves around this public mission.

Rather, as David Mathews and others have argued elsewhere, they have prioritized the professional mind-set and the culture of expertise over their commitment to public agency, public work, and public culture. In addition, colleges and universities have adopted a corporate model and embraced the market metaphor to define and package the product (education/knowledge) they provide. Students are customers to be served, who are paying high tuition dollars, to be credentialed to succeed in the market place. Increasingly, politicians and taxpayers are making direct correlations between the educational training offered by institutions of higher education and the economic development and vitality within the surrounding region. They want to see their tuition dollars and taxes deliver tangible products. The ideal of educating the public for democracy, providing the knowledge that undergirds government by the people, although still probably in many college and university mission statements, has long been replaced by market-driven concerns.

Also, I think this failure can be attributed to the larger cultural focus on defining public work in terms of volunteerism, charity, and service. In this way community work, civic engagement, and public agency are undermined and cast as philanthropy and benevolence. Volunteerism, service, and charity force public agency and civic engagement into an individualistic frame where the beneficent individual or institution bestows its knowledge and resources on needy communities as an act of love and concern, rather than as an integral part of building and sustaining democratic communities.

Yet, public universities currently face a real crisis as tuition costs rise and public funding falls. This is an opportune time to return to and revitalize the public missions of these institutions. I think what this means is that colleges and universities need to think consciously about their public agency and their role in the community. They need to reposition themselves as institutions that can facilitate and support public discourse—that can bring together diverse groups to deliberate and address community problems.

Brown: Do you think that universities such as yours can be open-ended in such work or do administrators, faculty and students expect more clarity from the outset?

Shaffer: This is very difficult, perhaps the most difficult part of this work. Community-based work does not fit neatly into the three-credit-hour course model, and it also doesn't fit neatly into the way administrators want to frame and assess learning objectives and outcomes. As the pressure increases to make institutions of higher education more accountable for the knowledge and skills they claim students are learning, administrators want faculty members to develop specific assignment rubrics with clear and measureable learning outcomes. This is difficult to do if you are truly honoring the partnership model. For partnerships to work they need to be fluid and flexible. Faculty and students need to be willing to change as the needs of the community change. Because faculty assessment focuses almost exclusively on scholarly publication and external grants, there is a significant and powerful emphasis on outcomes and fitting these outcomes into a framework that easily integrates into the faculty reward system. The case is similar with students. Since they have been socialized to think of education and knowledge as a kind of product or credential that will enhance their opportunities in the marketplace, they tend to think in terms of projects and end products—things that are easily documented and measured. All of these factors work against the need to be open-ended in community partnership work.

Brown: Are there really sufficient opportunities for students and faculty to experience collective work *with* others as distinguished from service *to* others?

Shaffer: This is a very important question. Acting Locally is specifically modeled to work in partnership with community members. We are very clear about the distinctions between service learning and community-based public work and scholarship. Although students in the Acting Locally program participate in service projects as part of learning about the communities they are interested in partnering with, they also are required to attend a range of community meetings, read local newspapers, meet with community representatives, conduct one on ones, engage in community asset mapping, research communities' histories, and a host of other experiences designed to foster public agency. Specifically, service-learning experiences lay the groundwork for our students to prepare for community asset mapping. But, the end goal is to develop, participate in, and sustain a relationship with a group of people in the community. We believe it is essential for students and faculty to see themselves as connected to communities and as active participants in the public work necessary to sustain diverse communities.

Brown: In general, do you think students find collective action more appealing than individual altruism?

Shaffer: My immediate answer is most definitely. But I think this is a complicated question. The dominant individualist culture values and validates public altruism and philanthropy over collective action. So, students and faculty are acknowledged and rewarded by the university for altruism over collective action. Giving, serving, and volunteering are strongly supported, better funded, and have much higher participation rates. Collective action and social advocacy are seen as too overtly political. Politics is still tainted with the polarization and bitterness of the culture wars. That said, those students I have worked with have been transformed by the public work they have engaged in.

Once students experience and begin to understand the difference between individual altruism and collective action, they begin to understand the possibilities of public engagement. Once they begin to make connections with the community and establish real relationships where they are sharing their knowledge and skills with community members in partnership, they begin to gain a sense of public agency, and they recognize the power of public work. In other words, they begin the process of moving beyond privatized and individualized cultural norms, they begin to think and act beyond themselves, and they begin to understand communities and their role in the community from a completely new perspective.

Brown: David Pelletier talks about the "ripple" effect in a community not easily traced or memorialized when participants in a partnership take some of what they've learned into their jobs, churches, and community life. Have you stories that confirm this ripple effect in the partnerships you pursue?

Shaffer: We are now just beginning course work with a new group of students. However, we are beginning to see these ripple effects. For example, last spring at the end the two-year curriculum, a group of students decided that the best way to sustain their community partnership, which involved a language exchange program between Miami students and members of the Latino community in Hamilton, Ohio, would be to create a student group. They worked with Associated Student Government (ASG) and set up a student organization called Student Activists for Language and Cultural Exchange (SALCE). As they note in their mission: "SALCE hopes to help make life in the United States more accessible to our non-English-speaking neighbors. As we form relationships and find ways to exercise community activism, we hope that we can help empower our region's immigrant community." They have created a Web site and recruited a whole new group of students to participate in the language exchange.

In rural Butler County, where students and faculty worked with the Miami Oxford Organic Network (MOON) Co-op to help support and build a local food economy, there have also been some ripple effects. The students helped compile and then published a rural food guide. Board members from the Oxford Farmers Market Uptown are now using the farmer biographies students wrote in their marketing materials to generate support for the farmers market and educate the community about the local farmers that serve them. In addition, one of our faculty members has partnered with a member of the Oxford Farmers Market Uptown to develop the Sprouts Program, which seeks to educate children aged 2-10 about local foods and to teach them how to grow food.

These are small steps. But I am hoping that as the Acting Locally program continues we will see more of these kinds of ripple effects.

CHAPTER FIVE

Higher Education Faculty and the Motivations of Civic Work

IF THERE IS REASON to be hopeful about higher education institutions and their democratic role, it is that faculty members are extremely passionate about their profession. Facing competitive job markets and modest salary scales, faculty are drawn to academia with the expectation that mentoring students and producing cutting-edge research will make a difference in society. The reality of higher education, however, can be extremely frustrating to these hopes. Scholars who chose their profession because it seemed to represent an honorable vocation are instead surprised to find that their work has little relevance beyond small circles of peer reviewers. They are confronted with hierarchical and bureaucratic institutions, and worst of all, citizens view their work with distrust. As a result, faculty appear to be experiencing a deep and widespread loss of what Arendt calls "public happiness," a sense of public relevance, across all disciplinary and institutional boundaries.[18] Symptomatic of a larger social shift, this separation between professional and civic identity extends across a range of fields, including journalism and philanthropy.

Nevertheless, the strongest critiques of politics as usual and the most innovative efforts to practice a new approach to higher education appear to be coming from higher education faculty. Some, using the concept of civic or democratic professionalism, go so far as to see their professional identity in explicitly political terms.[19] With little recognition from their disciplines or support from their institutions, this sense of professional identity appears to be the only plausible explanation for why academics persist in pursuing new forms of public scholarship and civic education, and the most promising source for a new kind of politics in higher education.

---

[18] Hannah Arendt, *On Revolution* (New York: Penguin, 1963; reprint, 1990), 127.

[19] Albert W. Dzur, *Democratic Professionalism: Citizen Participation and the Reconstruction of Professional Ethics, Identity, and Practice* (University Park: Pennsylvania State University Press, 2008).

Kettering's research on the civic aspects of faculty happiness and professional identity were the central theme of a 2004 occasional paper, *Going Public*, edited by Harry Boyte. One of the most resonant stories in that collection was that of Bill Doherty, a professor of family social science at the University of Minnesota. This piece speaks to the growing sense of a disconnect between the political ideals and professional practices of academics. The key moment in Doherty's transformation into professional work that builds civic capacities and catalyzes change in the community is the realization that his profession is "part of the problem."

IN 1985, I had my liberal progressive critique of materialism and consumerism in American culture well in place. I saw my world, the therapists' world, as the good guys. We were on the side of the angels.

I must have been open to some self-reflection. When I saw the review of *Habits of the Heart* by Robert Bellah and others in 1985, something told me it would be good for me to read it. I got the book to expand my critique of what was going on in American society, not to be challenged in my own work.

In one of the early chapters, the authors asked a therapist in California why she was committed to her children. She answered exactly the way I would have answered: "These are my values. I would feel guilty if I abandoned my children." The interviewers probed more deeply. "Would she want others to hold similar values?" She said, "Everyone has to choose their own values. It's not for me to impose values on others."

My hair stood up as I read this passage. I sat in the chair transfixed. It was shocking that this therapist could not speak in terms of public morality....

I don't know that I would have been any more articulate about my own values as a parent if they had asked me. But I realized that I had bought into the discourse of private psychology.

I was never the same. I realized that I and my profession were part of the problem, not just part of the solution to our country's social problems. I recently heard a presentation by four senior family therapy scholars who were regretting that they had not made more of their careers, having been buried in day-to-day teaching and clinical administration and worrying that their research had not made a difference for practitioners. I was sitting in the same room feeling fired up about my work, partly because I see myself as a catalyst and not as a "Lone Ranger." Some of the difference is inborn temperament (I got the optimistic Irish genes, not the depressive ones), but some of it is working with a different paradigm. Citizenship work has transformed my career and renewed the sense of idealism that brought me to this field.

Communitarianism was a good model to start from in the 1980s, a both/and, private/public philosophy. I had discovered Amitai Etzioni and Alan Wolfe and other communitarian thinkers while writing my book *Soul Searching.*

A colleague and I discussed what a citizen therapist would actually do in the world. We created "salons," or Networker Forums outside Minnesota, in an effort to create a collective way for therapists to think about these issues. It turns out, in retrospect, that the reason people often joined these forum groups was that they were feeling frustrated about managed care. They really were not into the community part of therapy. But these groups also tapped into the idealism of therapists who had entered the field in the '60s. At the initial organizing meetings, people talked in an agonized way, planning to change the world. They would say, "Then, I settled into private practice. I wanted to put my kids through college. I'm so exhausted at the end of the week I don't have time to volunteer. And now managed care is boxing me in."

I didn't have the words for it, but I knew something was missing from how we were all thinking about ourselves as citizens and professionals.... I began to read about public work—professional practice that is politically energizing, catalytic, civically educative, and politically effective. It helped me develop a conceptual framework for action as a therapist. I had been giving talks to a variety of community groups about strengthening family life. The action breakthrough was in Wayzata, Minnesota, in April 1998.

I talked with a large group of parents at a parent fair. The parents were lit up over the problem of feeling out of control of their time but afraid to get off the treadmill. A middle school principal said, "We're part of this problem. We offer so many activities to kids that if parents agree to half of them, they're not going to have much of a family life left."

That was the dawning for me that this issue of overscheduling was not just an individual family issue and a cultural issue. It was a structural issue as well. I talked to other people. Light bulbs started coming on for them and me both. Family time is a public issue.

A couple of months later, the organizer of the original parent fair asked me to come back next year and give that talk again. That was the moment that I decided to go for it. I turned her down. "I don't want to give Doherty's greatest hits. But if you want to take on this problem as a community, I've been learning a model to do this, and I'd be willing to come back and work with you to figure out how to do it."

We organized a town meeting for the following spring. About 70 people, including parents, school board people, and community leaders, came. These people were ready. I began by asking, "Are these things we are talking about here—overscheduled kids and underconnected families—only individual family problems or are they also community problems? Are the solutions only individual family solutions, or are they also community solutions? What can we do about the problems as a community?"

It was an electrifying experience. When it was over, participants had decided to do something about the problem and, among other things, formed a community activation team. That group ultimately became the steering group for Family Life First. Putting Family Life First became an organization that works to reclaim family life from a hyperactive consumer culture. It now has several affiliates and has sparked a national conversation and debate about family overscheduling.

Civic work in academia results from a range of both intellectual and political motivations. In this piece, Adam Weinberg, Executive Vice President of World Learning, reflects on the path he took to his previous position, Dean of the College at Colgate University, where he worked to make civic education a top institutional priority. Weinberg describes the central role of his passions for community organizing and intellectual life in the development of his professional identity. These reflections were part of an interview conducted by David Brown for *HEX* (2006) and republished in *Agent of Democracy*.

Brown: To start off, Adam, can you describe the work that you have been doing at Colgate?

Weinberg: It has been a seven-year process to rebuild campus life at Colgate around principles of civic learning. We started by getting about 400 students involved in a partnership with the local community around economic development. We did everything from work on a microenterprise program to help develop a "buy local" campaign. That work led to about $15 million of investment in the local community. We then launched an innovative community center to move students from thin forms of service to deeper forms of team-based community work. Based on lessons learned from the community work, we launched our residential education program, which has gotten a lot of national attention. The basic idea was to "capture all the educational moments" that take place as students' time on campus. We have focused on capturing the civic potential in residential halls, student organizations, and other forms of everyday life....

Brown: You mentioned getting national attention. What is the significance of the work you describe?

Weinberg: ... At Colgate, we have moved away from a professional service model by infusing campus with the spirit of public work. We want students to think of themselves as members of a community who have a responsibility to work with others to create a healthy living environment. We are then working with them to make sure that they have the organizing skills to act on their public values.

In my view, there are a few important shifts embedded in this view: first, we are arguing that we need to give students a more robust definition of democracy that moves beyond democracy as voting and community service to democracy as a way of life. To get to this place, we need to capture all the educational moments. Civic education takes place in campus controversies, residential halls, student organizations, campus planning, and a range of other places. Finally, we are challenging people to move beyond values. We need to make sure that our students have the skills and habits to act on their values.

Brown: Faculty involvement seems to have been an important part of all that you and others have done. Given the habits and priorities of faculty, have there been significant changes in the degree of their participation?

Weinberg: Yes. More faculty are aware of what we are doing and helpful in articulating the message and support with students. And more faculty are involved in programs and (more important) in planning.... They are trying to ensure that we are thinking broadly across the totality of what we are doing. We also have faculty heavily involved in other programs. A few have even offered to live in our residential halls!

Perhaps the most important involvement has been the very informal ways faculty mentor students. As one would expect, our faculty spend lots of time with students in their offices talking about all sorts of things. As part of this, faculty have been really important in helping change the culture. One of the hardest parts of the shift is getting students to understand a changed set of expectations for college life. Faculty are involved in helping explain the message.

It is also interesting, however, that faculty have not driven this process. There is a division of labor that works for us.... Faculty are engaged in research that really matters to moving society forward. I would argue that we need faculty to worry about how to do civic education through the classroom with more engaged pedagogies (e.g. problem-based learning, service learning, community-based research). We need student affairs folks to worry about doing this through things like residential programs and student organizations. And we need student affairs and academic affairs leaders (e.g. administrators and faculty idea entrepreneurs) to be talking/coordinating with each other.

Brown: When we spoke earlier you said that it is easy to justify civic education within the context of the liberal arts. If so, why then has the classroom been a problem?

Weinberg: Part of it is real. Faculty have multiple demands on their time. They have lots of competing needs for the classroom. Part of it is new. We are just starting to understand the power of engaged pedagogies. That requires constructing structures with incentives to help faculty stay on the cutting edge of teaching.

But part of it is also less real, or self-imposed in destructive ways. Too many faculty have professionalized themselves. They see themselves as a narrow type of scientist. My father was a scientist. I often find it odd that many faculty in the social sciences are trying to be a sort of scientist that most scientists would not want to be. Great civic education comes from faculty who think about themselves, their work, and their teaching in much more craft-like ways. My discipline (sociology) may be the worst. As we become more professionalized we have less to offer students and more irrelevant to larger public conversations. Given the history of sociology, we should see lots of sociologists interested in civic education and/or service learning. Instead, sociologists are scared that it will make them seem "weak" or "not a real scientist."

Brown: In the "Social Change" piece you mention the "generation of faculty moving into deans' positions who came of age in the movements of the '60s."[20] Does that describe your own journey? Did you become "disillusioned and professionalized" along the way? Did you "retool your professional obligations"? Could you tell me more about that journey?

---

[20]Adam Weinberg, "The University: An Agent of Social Change?" *Qualitative Sociology*, Volume 25, Number 2 (2002): 263-272.

Weinberg: I was born in 1965, so I am too young. My journey is probably more typical of the younger academics, who are becoming associate faculty and taking on administrative roles. I came into the academy because everybody was going to graduate school and I didn't want to go to law school. I was searching for a way to combine different passions: community organizing, writing, the world of ideas. I was also looking for a profession that would allow me to live my politics. I wanted an egalitarian marriage.

I was also driven into the academy by a passion for democracy. I wanted to spend my life working on ways to make communities (the places people live) more democratic. That is why I was attracted to community-based research and service learning. I wanted to raise my children in a social and political household. I probably would have left graduate school had community-based research and service learning not become acceptable ways of doing things. It gave me ways to combine my passions for community work with my love for writing and thinking. I stayed because I came to understand the untapped potential of universities. Along the way, I fell deeply in love with teaching.

Over time, I have become more optimistic and less professionalized. I see my work as a craft. I came very close to leaving the academy a few years ago. I had viewed myself as an academic who was focused externally. I had never envisioned myself as an administrator. I actually thought that I would be one of those people who moved back and forth between the nonprofit/government to university worlds. But, I became excited by academic administration. I came to work for a great college president, Rebecca Chopp....

... When an institution takes up public work/civic education as a driving principle you can achieve amazing results on students, faculty research, community development, alumni, and parents, and even helping to shape the agendas of foundations and trade associations. In my current role, I was able to advocate that civic learning become a top priority for Colgate. We are on the verge of universities becoming more relevant ... or we could be.... I wanted to be part of that process. I also see management as another arena of public work. In three years, we have managed to deprofessionalize our student affairs division, recentering it around notions of public work. This is my own way of thinking about and contributing to a "democracy through the workplace" movement.

In this piece, David Brown asks KerryAnn O'Meara, Associate Professor of Higher Education to help account for the emergence of civic work among faculty, despite institutional cultures and reward systems that do little to encourage the public sides of their professional identities.

Brown: You speak of faculty members *learning* in their respective community engagement experiences. What do they expect to learn and what do they actually learn?

O'Meara: Over the last few years I have become very familiar with the work of Anna Neumann of Teachers College on faculty learning and it very much influenced a new ASHE monograph that I, Aimee Terosky, and Anna Neumann have coming out in fall 2008 on faculty growth in their professional lives. Neumann posits that learning really should be considered at the center of faculty work. Whether in their teaching, research, or as university citizens, faculty are expected to be "master learners." Like students, faculty learning is going to be influenced by their social environments and by what they bring to them.

While I think faculty rarely articulate or position themselves as learners in a given situation or part of their work, learning draws them in and is embedded in the most passionate parts of their work. For example, in the last two decades many faculty have become involved in what is often referred to as the scholarship of teaching—or studying their teaching practice. They study how what they do and what their students do facilitate learning as well as reflect on their own learning in the classroom. You can always find in the work of such scholar-teachers, stories that show how much they love the classroom, how much possibility they feel that it has, and how much they want to understand and actualize that potential. I would add that for myself—I find I am most creative when trying to craft a class that will be interesting for my students and really guide their learning. I think this is because I am learning myself about the material in new ways as I prepare each session.

Likewise, Anna Neumann did some work on the passion involved in research, and she found faculty talking about when they were in the "zone" per se with their work—when they felt most alive and felt real joy in discovery. Similarly, I think faculty involved in public work often want to learn something related to their discipline and how certain things work in the world. However, often they find that pursuit of one kind of learning leads to another set of learning.

Brown: For example ...

O'Meara: For example, often to learn the knowledge they need they have to acquire skills in how to disseminate information in ways that catalyze as opposed to paralyze publics, or networking skills, or grant writing or public speaking or even writing for lay audiences skills. In addition, I think the more engaged they become in public issues, the more their identity and professional orientation starts to become reshaped. In short, I think faculty can learn new knowledge (such as the cultural issues behind a child obesity problem in a community), skills (such as learning to work well with people from other disciplines), as well as professional orientation (such as a sense of being part of a collective of people responsible for addressing the situation).

Brown: Does this point back to a faculty member's graduate school experience? You point out that [there] are "few opportunities for graduate students to learn the knowledge sets, skills, and orientation specific to [community] engagement within their discipline." What specific changes need to be made in graduate school education to address your concern?

O'Meara: One of my points of entry into the conversation about what needs to happen to prepare graduate students to be engaged scholars has been my experiences with reward systems. Most faculty are not socialized to think about engaged teaching and research in graduate school at all, much less to consider ways in which it could be meaningful and rigorous in their discipline. As a result, they enter a personnel committee and sit there to evaluate the work of an engaged scholar and are either completely biased against it or open, but feel unprepared to judge its quality.

However, if the faculty in each graduate department made a collective attempt to consider how their work connected to the public, if they went so far as to commit to having public partners we could expose an entire new generation of future faculty to engagement and public work.

Brown: But is it realistic that such a "commitment" will emerge given the way faculty are educated?

O'Meara: It is often not in the best interest of a faculty member to be involved in public work as a "Lone Ranger," but rather as a collective department or enclave committed to opening up their part of an institution to public issues. I say this for reasons of promotion and tenure and a base of support for the work–the more folks involved, the more who will support you and get it. Also, commitments by a department to particular community or public partnerships are more likely to be institutionalized in ways that last longer than individuals who eventually retire and often do not have the power to hire their replacements.

However, a deeper structural barrier to faculty work as "public" relates to the foundation upon which faculty work rests. While of course this differs by institutional type, the pedestal or foundation upon which faculty do much of their work is considered by most to be innately private.

Imagine an umbrella. There is the handle and long stick at the center. From this central foundation come spokes which branch out and support the top material. Building on this metaphor, the central stick and spokes are similar to the foundation of a faculty career, such as their appointment in a discipline or unit of a college or university. This appointment is made with an understanding of accountability to an essentially private interest–the effective running of that department or unit, and in a broader way the college. The more research oriented the unit, the more the unit will call upon disciplinary peers outside the institution, to make sure that person's work is accountable to their private interest–that that person is cutting edge in their research in the field. The more teaching oriented, the more that unit will hold the faculty member accountable to teaching evaluations from "private, paying students" and advising and service work to the unit. In either case though, the unit holds the faculty member accountable to their own interests through reappointment to contracts, tenure, and promotion. It then becomes in that faculty member's self interest to be reappointed and promoted by serving the interests of that unit. This encourages the spokes that come off the central stick—that is, the teaching, research, and service to be more private activities—in that they are accountable only to the interests of their units.

What this means is that even when faculty engage in excellent public work, such as the example Bill Doherty gives, it is in many ways also private work. That is, the faculty member decided to do the work, and may have public partners in it, but is not accountable for it at the core of their appointment. Rather, it is considered something nice that they do as a sort of social entrepreneur on top of their appointment rather than as something core to their appointments. It is not considered central to their appointments or roles.

What this structure means is that the public comes to think of 90 percent of what faculty do as private work. They are educating someone else's children, or mine only because I am paying them as I would a financial advisor for a service. Research is considered something faculty do to get tenure, not something that relates to my grandmother with Alzheimer's.

Brown: Assuming the commitment you speak of can emerge, what form do you think it should take in graduate education?

O'Meara: Research and the experiences of engaged scholars suggest it is more effective and sustainable for entire departments, or enclaves of faculty, to engage in this work together than as individuals. In graduate education we typically gain and develop knowledge, skills, and a professional orientation. If a department were to come together and find ways to invite even one or two community partners into their programs, there would be opportunities for graduate students to develop knowledge, skills, and a professional orientation in new ways. For example, the program and community partners could obtain grants together that allow students to do work in the field as part of their studies. There could be teaching opportunities that bring community partners into the classroom and faculty and students into the public realm. Joint research projects could be disseminated to both public and academic audiences as students learn skills about how to communicate to both audiences simultaneously. These community partner, student, and faculty colleagues can teach each other about developing questions and seeking answers in their field and build on prior knowledge while also being immediately relevant to public interests.

Brown: Do trustees of a particular institution have a role in using "rewards" to develop the commitment you speak of?

O'Meara: I have been thinking a lot lately about this question in terms of some of the reasons faculty work overall is not more public, or seen as more public. The nature of the question itself is telling, because of course most public institutions historically were created by state, region, and town "publics." Even many small private liberal arts colleges were founded by public citizens, with public money to educate their sons and daughters, to create libraries available to the citizens of that area, and to bring different kinds of culture in terms of the arts to more rural areas. Today most public, and many private higher education institutions, have boards of trustees that are made up of citizens of that state and/or region as well as alumni, business CEOs, politically appointed members, etc. This board of trustees, in public institutions at least, is supposed to watch out for the public interest in the running of the university or state college. Yet all too often the role of the board of trustees becomes fundraising and not a preoccupation with representing the public interest in how the institution is run on a daily basis.

Brown: Should there be new governance structures where members of a community are included?

O'Meara: I think whether it be private or public institutions, the way to encourage more faculty work to be public in nature is to rethink the foundation upon which their positions rest. It would also mean rethinking the level at which community members have roles in institutions. There is much to learn from community colleges, who often have public citizens involved in institutional decision making at a more local level and also from efforts to make Teaching As Community Property, taken by the Carnegie Foundation.

Brown: We both like Julie Ellison's wonderful metaphor she uses for the "shuttle-zone" between the academy and the public "as a ferry working its way back and forth between two banks of a river moving people, things, languages, ideas." I know "the ferry" carries students and faculty to the public shore, but, from your perspective, is there good reason for the public to cross to the academic shore?

O'Meara: Absolutely. If we think of higher education at its best as being a set of opportunities, opportunities that can be transformative—then waiting on the banks and in the halls, and throughout the space of the college or university is literally almost limitless potential. I know this sounds optimistic—but I have often been involved in service-learning programs that bring future first-generation students to colleges to look at the class-rooms, the recreation centers, the residence halls; to meet faculty; etc. and you see it so much when you look at their faces taking it all in—this awe and joy at what it might be like to be there, to belong there, to have this be their world. Likewise, each mayor, or local doctor, or community organizer or teacher or political candidate or engineer that visits our classrooms or coauthors our research takes part in a process of claiming that space as more public, sort of decreasing elitism and remaking the space as ours—academic and nonacademic together—rather than theirs. One of the reasons the ferry image works so well is also because the pathway is flat—rather than the uni-versity being on a hill. Both groups need to go back and forth. However, I think we really need to work on the "ports" on either side—to make them inviting and easier to navigate and more welcoming.

Brown: What motivates faculty engaged in civic work? It's not the cur-rent reward structure, and it's not ego, because civic work requires academ-ics to question their own claim to expertise. So what makes them tick?

O'Meara: I recently did a study of the personal narratives of engaged fac-ulty nominated for the Campus Compact Ehrlich award.[21] I found faculty motivated by a variety of factors including but not limited to a desire to facili-tate student learning through service learning, to achieve disciplinary goals, personal commitments to community or social issues or causes, professional identity as public scholars, a desire for what Scott Peters and others discuss as "public making," and last a desire to fulfill an institutional or department college mission.

What I think is very telling and fits in with my comments earlier is that most of these motivations are inherently intrinsic—it is the faculty member's decision. Even in the case of institutional mission, the faculty member is likely in a place where public work is just one of many ways that they could help fulfill mission and they chose this one. High course and advising loads leave less discretionary time in two-year colleges, and yet there are still

---

[21] KerryAnn O'Meara, "Motivation for Faculty Community Engagement: Learning from Examples," *Journal of Higher Education Outreach and Engagement*, 12:1 (2008).

opportunities to decide where one might make contributions to mission and to the public.

Because the motivations for public work are inherently sewn into the personal and professional narrative of ourselves, this work often occurs outside of, or as Harry Boyte says, upstream against, reward systems. While more and more campuses have worked to assess this work as forms of scholarship and include it in their reward systems, my work with faculty suggests that for faculty most engaged and evolved in the work, this is nice confirmation but not central to the "why" of their work. Faculty are in fact "getting" many things out of this work—including a sense that what they study and do everyday matters in the world, real partners in efforts that are important to them, tools to teach students better, and often new and fresher ways to look at issues in their disciplines.

This may not be the "currency" that peer-reviewed articles in top-tier journals or significant grant funding bring, but it is a powerful currency and set of assets on its own that we may often overlook when we ask, why do this?

Afterword: Ships Passing in the Night?

MARGUERITE SHAFFER, director of American studies at Miami University, is one of a surprisingly large number of faculty members who are at odds with an academic culture that isn't hospitable to their efforts to combine a public life with a scholarly career. She is concerned about what is happening in her field and about the world her two children will inherit. I have often quoted what she said in an interview for the 2008 issue of the *Higher Education Exchange* because it captures so well what troubles other faculty:

> I have joked with colleagues that I am in the midst of an academic midlife crisis—questioning every aspect of life in academe. In thinking about my future in the university, I have wondered whether my time will be well spent researching and writing a scholarly monograph that might well get me promoted, but that will be read by only a handful of like-minded scholars with similar intellectual interests. I have questioned the time I devote to teaching critical thinking skills to students who are socialized, both inside and outside the university, to care more about their final grades and potential career options than the knowledge they can share and the collective future they will create.

The Shaffers of academe are one of the forces driving a civic engagement movement on campuses across the country. Not so long ago, the civic education of college students was of little concern. Now, thanks to educators like Shaffer, that indifference is giving way. Leadership programs are common, and students are taught civic skills, including civil dialogue. There are also more opportunities to be of service these days, which is socially beneficial as well as personally rewarding. These opportunities are enriched by students' exposure to the political problems behind the needs that volunteers try to meet. University partnerships with nearby communities offer technical assistance, professional advice, and access to institutional resources. Faculty, who were once "sages on the stage," have learned to be more effective in communities by being "guides on the side." All in all, there is much to admire in the civic engagement movement on campuses.

Another civic engagement movement is occurring off campus. At Kettering, we have seen it clearly in communities on the Gulf Coast that are recovering from Hurricane Katrina. We have combined what we learned from several communities into a fictional composite in order to report from across the region. In this representative community, "Don" and his wife, "Mary," live in an old fishing village much like Bayou La Batre, Alabama. The community traces its origins back to an 18th-century French settlement, and Don's family has been there since 1831. Mary came from Pennsylvania for a vacation—and stayed—as have other northern transplants. The residents of the community include Creoles descended from French and West African ancestors, as well as a large group of fishermen who recently arrived from Southeast Asia. There have been some tensions among these different groups but, fortunately, no serious clashes.

The hurricane destroyed a good many houses, and Don and Mary are still living with relatives in the area. Their hardware store was damaged, though not badly, and they were able to reopen within a year. Business is slow, however, because many people left for less vulnerable areas of the state. The fishing industry was hit very hard; boats were blown inland, and it took considerable effort to get them back into the water. Fishing is a competitive business, yet most families pitched in to help one another. When the schoolhouse collapsed, churches that survived made space available for classes while a new building was being constructed. Don volunteers at the local fire station, which received supplies from a station in another small town two states away. This assistance was critical while waiting for state and federal support to arrive. Crime has gone up, but the police chief has begun a program of community-assisted policing, which he hopes will be effective if neighbors will participate.

The big news is that outside developers, aided by a planning grant from the state development office, are considering buying up a large tract of land just south of the town limits. They intend to build a "world class resort." Some people see prosperity just around the corner; others worry that the developers will dominate the reconstruction and shut them out of the decision making about the community's future. This prompted some concerned citizens to meet every week at the fire station to develop their own plans for the town. People wanted to restore their community—both its buildings and way of life—and felt that they had to come together as a community to do that. The community was both their objective and the means of reaching that objective. This has been the goal for many of the other civic engagement movements in communities that are trying to cope with natural disasters, economic change, and other problems that threaten everyone's well-being.

Interestingly, a year or so after Katrina, a group of scholars studying communities that survived disasters validated the instincts of Don, Mary, and their neighbors. These communities were resilient because they had developed the capacity to come together. And the resilience proved more important than individual protective measures like well-stocked pantries.[22]

People with a democratic bent like Don, Mary, and their neighbors don't want to be informed, organized, or assisted as much as they want to be in charge of their lives. And they sense that this means they need a greater capacity to act together despite their differences. That is why they say they want to come together as communities to maintain their communities. Unfortunately, they often have difficulty finding institutions that understand their agenda.

---

[22] Monica Schoch-Spana et al., "Community Engagement: Leadership Tool for Catastrophic Health Events," *Biosecurity and Bioterrorism: Biodefense Strategy, Practice, and Science* 5, no. 1 (2007): 8-25; and Paloma Dallas, "Studies of a Role for Communities in the Face of Catastrophe," *Connections* (2008): 31-34.

Nongovernmental organizations, according to a recent Kettering and Harwood study, are often more interested in demonstrating the impact of *their* programs than in facilitating self-determination and self-rule.[23] Even citizens may be uncertain of what they can do by themselves and want to put the responsibility on schools, police departments, or other government agencies. For instance, in one community, citizens decided that there weren't enough adult mentors for the young people who were getting into trouble. Yet rather than identifying places where youngsters could find adults within the community who would be responsive, these citizens wanted social workers to handle the problem.

The Wetlands of Democracy

Prompted by what we *don't* know about communities coming together, the Kettering Foundation has begun to collect stories and analyze case studies.[24] One of the first things we learned from people like Don, Mary, and their neighbors is that they absolutely refused to call what they were doing "politics." They wanted to distinguish what they were about from what goes on in elections and governments, although they usually voted and weren't rabid critics of the government.

We don't have a name for what we are seeing, but the more we see, the more we have come to believe that we are looking at something more than civil society at work, more than revitalized public life, and more than grassroots initiatives. We don't think we are seeing an alternative political system like direct democracy; rather, we are looking at the roots of self-rule. Democratic politics seems to operate at two levels. The most obvious is the institutional level, which includes elections, lawmaking, and the delivery of services. The other level is underneath these superstructures, and what happens there is much like what happens in the wetlands of a natural ecosystem.

---

[23]Richard C. Harwood and John A. Creighton, *The Organization-First Approach: How Communities Get Crowded Out* (Dayton, OH: Kettering Foundation and The Harwood Institute for Public Innovation, 2008).

[24]The foundation's findings have been reported in *For Communities to Work* (Dayton, OH: Kettering Foundation, 2002) and more recently in *Engaging Citizens: Meeting the Challenges of Community Life* (Dayton, OH: Kettering Foundation, October 2006).

We have been experimenting with a wetlands analogy to describe what supports and sustains institutional politics. Wetlands were once overlooked and unappreciated but were later recognized as the nurseries for marine life. For example, the swamps along the Gulf Coast were filled in by developers, and the barrier islands were destroyed when boat channels were dug through them. The consequences were disastrous. Sea life that bred in the swamps died off, and coastal cities were exposed to the full fury of hurricanes when the barrier islands eroded. The wetlands of politics play roles similar to swamps and barrier islands. They include informal gatherings, ad hoc associations, and the seemingly innocuous banter that goes on when people mull over the meaning of their everyday experiences. These appear inconsequential when compared with what happens in elections, legislative bodies, and courts. Yet mulling over the meaning of everyday experiences in grocery stores and coffee shops can be the wellspring of public decision making. Connections made in these informal gatherings become the basis for political networks, and ad hoc associations evolve into civic organizations.[25]

In the political wetlands, as in institutional politics, problems are given names, issues are framed for discussion, decisions are made, resources are identified and utilized, actions are organized, and results are evaluated. In politics at both levels, action is taken or not; power is generated or lost; change occurs or is blocked. We aren't watching perfect democracy in the political wetlands because there isn't such a thing. But we are seeing ways of acting, of generating power, and of creating change that are unlike what occurs in institutional politics.

Recently, we have been calling these characteristics "organic." Like any generalization, this one has its drawbacks. Still, we were drawn to the term, in part, because it doesn't have the varied meanings of words like *civic* and *public*. The word *organic* connotes things that are natural or close to ordinary life, things that are human and function like living organisms. That which is organic is also loosely structured, more like a blob than a square or, in political terms, more informal than formal. There are other qualities that seem to

---

[25]The Harwood Group, *Meaningful Chaos: How People Form Relationships with Public Concerns* (Dayton, OH: Kettering Foundation, 1993).

be unique to organic politics:

- Citizens are defined by their relationships with other citizens rather than with the state.
- Relationships are not the same as those of family and friends, yet they are unlike those in institutional politics, which may be based on patronage or party loyalty. Organic relationships are pragmatic or work related. They form when people coalesce in order to rescue and restore during a disaster, when they build houses for the homeless, or when they assist the police in watching for drug dealers in their neighborhoods.
- The names people give to problems reflect the things they hold dear and their basic concerns—their highest hopes and deepest fears as human beings. Safety from danger. Being treated fairly. The freedom to act as they see best. These names are different from those that people use when they are acting as professionals and politicians. For example, citizens want to feel that they are safe in their homes, and this feeling of security is less quantifiable but more compelling than the statistics professionals use to describe crime.
- The knowledge needed to decide what to do about these problems is created in the cauldron of collective decision making. It is formed by the interaction of people with other people, by the comparison of experience with experience. This knowledge is different from the way scholarly knowledge is created, which is through rigorously disciplined science.
- Decisions are based on the recognition that concerns are interrelated as well as competing, which is not the assumption in majority voting. Organic decision making is deliberative. Deliberation involves carefully weighing possible actions against what people consider most valuable, which has to be determined in a specific context. Institutional decision making can also be deliberative, although it is more often based on negotiation and bargaining.
- The resources needed to implement decisions come from citizens' innate abilities, abilities that are magnified when people join in collective efforts. Citizens' resources are often intangible, such as commitment and political will. These are different from the resources of institutions, which tend to be material and technical.

- The citizenry acts in various ways, which are loosely coordinated by a shared sense of direction. Actions taken by institutions are usually uniform and directed by a single plan or central agency.
- The commitment of resources to action is enforced by covenants or the promises people make to one another. Institutional commitments are enforced by legal contracts.
- Power comes from the ability of citizens to make things through their collective efforts and from the relationships forged in these efforts, rather than from institutional authority.
- Change comes about through collective learning and the innovation it generates, rather than from modifications of law and policy.

Organic politics has its own structures: not board tables but kitchen tables, not assemblies like legislative bodies but common gatherings, once in post office lobbies but now on the Internet. These structures are more like sand than concrete. Ad hoc groups and alliances form, then fall away as a project is completed, but reappear when another task is at hand.

Why the Disconnect?

It would seem that two civic engagement movements, occurring at the same time and often in the same locations, would be closely allied—perhaps mutually reinforcing. That doesn't seem to be happening very often. Research reported by Sean Creighton in the 2008 issue of the *Higher Education Exchange* suggests the connection is quite limited. Even though academic institutions have considerable expertise and a genuine interest in being helpful, they don't necessarily know how to relate to the self-organizing impulses of Don, Mary, and their neighbors.

Creighton found that few university-community initiatives "focused on building relationships with community partners, much less on projects that increased the civic capacity of those community organizations and the individuals they served." There are exceptions, of course. But, by and large, we have found that the emphasis is on institutions *serving* communities better by listening carefully and communicating more clearly.

Academics and neighborhood associations are quite aware of power differences between them, and universities often try to share institutional power; that is, to "empower" citizens. Yet, communicating with, serving, and empowering communities isn't the same as building indigenous civic capacity—the capacity of a citizenry to join forces and act.

One study isn't enough to generalize about all types of partnerships, so the Creighton report is more of a caution light than a stop sign. Efforts by colleges and universities to reach outside their walls is certainly a positive development. Too much benefit has come from the service provided by academic institutions to take their contribution lightly.

Why, though, are these two civic movements in danger of passing like the proverbial ships in the night? More important, how might these efforts become mutually supportive? One reason may be that like the natural wetlands, the value of the political wetlands isn't easily recognized.

Because politics in the wetlands appears insignificant or deficient by institutional standards, professional staffs tend to colonize democracy at this level and remake it in their own image. The mechanisms for doing this are well intended and familiar: empowerment projects, participatory mandates, accountability standards, and engagement campaigns. These build support for deserving institutions (like public schools), promote better understanding of government agencies, and provide institutional legitimacy. Their goal is to connect citizens to institutions; yet, in the rush to do that, the need for citizens to *first* engage one another is often overlooked.

Fixation on institutional politics may be another factor in obscuring the significance of what happens in the larger ecosystem of democracy. And this fixation may contribute to lack of discussion of the various kinds of democracy that are being promoted by both on- and off-campus engagement projects. One common reaction to the variety of initiatives in civic education, for instance, is to think of them as competing methodologies serving the same end. In fact, these campus projects may reflect very different notions of democracy, particularly different concepts of the role of citizens.

Some colleges and universities insist they serve democracy simply by existing. Maybe so, but what *kind* of democracy? Even when academics use the same terminology, they may not have the same concepts of democracy in mind. As reported in the 2006 issue of the *Higher Education Exchange*, Derek Barker found five distinct practices all using the same generic label, the scholarship of engagement.

Nothing is wrong with this variety; nonetheless, wouldn't it be beneficial if the concepts of democracy in different projects were made more explicit? One of the characteristics of democracy is a vigorous debate over its meaning. A crucial distinction needs to be made between projects that address the problems *in* a democracy (violence, injustice, poverty) and those that deal with the problems *of* democracy (moral disagreement, polarization, alienation). Both kinds are worthwhile, yet the problems of democracy may be getting less attention. If so, the potential in making use of what happens in the wetlands of democracy will remain unrecognized.

One indication that the problems of democracy aren't visible is the way that deliberative democracy has been interpreted. The recent attention given to the important role deliberation plays in democracy has come about because of a serious problem of democracy—how to justify or make legitimate decisions when there are significant moral disagreements over which decisions are best. Deliberation is key because it takes into account the things that are held valuable, which gives rise to moral disagreements. That is a far cry from the way public deliberation is often understood today, which is merely as one of many techniques used to promote civil discourse. We could certainly do with a little more civility in our political rhetoric—but public deliberation is far more than a methodology for ensuring politeness. It is an essential element in a democracy in which citizens are actors producing public goods.

Make no mistake; anytime there are moral disagreements, emotions will flare. That happens in deliberations. Far from suppressing emotions, deliberations recognize and help people work through strong feelings. The objective is to make sound decisions that have legitimacy because the concerns that produce the emotions have been recognized. Although not resulting in total agreement, deliberation helps people find enough common ground to act together. By doing this, it enables citizens to become effective political actors.

One of the most powerful insights to come from deliberative forums is the political power available in seemingly trivial activities, like giving names to problems that need to be solved. When people fail to see names for problems that reflect their personal experiences and what they value, they feel outside the political system looking in. On the other hand, when people deliberate, they usually rename problems in their own terms. They claim the power inherent in owning their problems.

Moving On

The challenge higher education faces is to not let its engagement movement stall; one way to do that is to align its efforts more closely with those of Don, Mary, and their neighbors. Some colleges and universities are already beginning to do this. Kettering doesn't know about all of these initiatives, so I can only draw from a few examples we have information on.

As already mentioned, citizens don't necessarily see the potential in the wetlands of democracy or the power that comes from joining forces with other citizens. An experiment on the Wake Forest campus has broken through that barrier with a four-year program that gave students a better sense of how they can become effective political actors, not just on election day, but every day. [26] Two faculty members, Katy Harriger and Jill McMillan, introduced deliberative democracy as a way of doing politics. Deliberative forums were organized at multiple sites: in classrooms, in the campus community, and in the town where the university is located. Deliberation wasn't presented as just a way of conducting forums, but as a way of living democratically.

This experiment shows that deliberative democracy challenges academic institutions at every level: from the nature of teaching and the character of the extracurricular program to the very meaning of scholarship. Perhaps the greatest challenge is epistemological. Deliberation creates morally relevant public knowledge about what is most important to people's collective well-

---

[26] That experiment is documented in Katy J. Harriger and Jill J. McMillan, *Speaking of Politics: Preparing College Students for Democratic Citizenship through Deliberative Dialogue* (Dayton, OH: Kettering Foundation Press, 2007).

being. This knowledge has to be socially constructed by citizens; it is neither better nor worse than expert, scientific knowledge, just different. The role of public knowledge (perhaps better called practical wisdom) is to generate sound judgments about what should be done in politics. How institutions of higher education contribute to this knowledge, which people need to rule themselves wisely, is an open question.

On another front, a new coalition of cooperative extension folks is taking on the challenge of finding ways to strengthen the democratic capacities in organic politics in order to form resilient, self-governing communities. We can hope that this coalition will be able to better align the ways their institutions go about their business with the way citizens go about theirs.

Still another group of initiatives is emerging from more than 40 centers and institutes that have sprung up around the country using public deliberation to give people direct experience with organic politics. Some promote deliberative forums to make the collective decisions that are needed to launch collective action on state and local problems. Others use the forums to combat the polarization that creates stalemates in our policymaking. These forums, often based on the National Issues Forums series of issue books, look at the pros and cons of three or more possible courses of action on controversial issues like abortion, race relations, and environmental protection.

Some of these institutes, such as the ones at Hofstra and Kansas State, are embedded in their universities. Others are freestanding, like the one in Alabama, and have ties to several universities. A number of institutes, including the one at the University of Hawaii, have strong connections to state legislatures. Still others are embedded in their communities but collaborate with a nearby university, as is the case for Penn State and the ad hoc Public Issues Forums of Centre County group.

Whether its these 40 plus centers and institutes, the cooperative extension coalition, experiments in undergraduate education like the one at Wake Forest, or other initiatives I haven't mentioned here, higher education is not only keeping its civic engagement movement going but also giving that movement a stronger democratic cast. The academy is bringing its efforts more in line with the efforts of people who want to do the work of citizens.

This publication hopes to contribute to this alignment, which has the potential to stimulate fresh conceptual insights and tap into new reservoirs of civic energy.

We need more opportunities on and off campus for Marguerite Shaffer and her colleagues to meet with Don, Mary, and their neighbors, not as service providers and recipients, but as coproducers of democracy. The exchange can also help academic institutions renew their sense of themselves. Colleges and universities are more than knowledge factories to be judged solely by their efficiency. From the American Revolution through the civil rights movement, they have been part of the greatest experiment of all, an experiment based on the proposition that we, citizens, can actually govern ourselves.

David Mathews, President
Kettering Foundation

CONTRIBUTORS

DEREK W. M. BARKER is a program officer at the Kettering Foundation. He works primarily on research concerning the democratic role of higher education institutions and professionals. He is the author of *Tragedy and Citizenship: Conflict, Reconciliation, and Democratic Politics from Haemon to Hegel* (SUNY Press, 2008). He holds a PhD in political science from Rutgers University and previously taught at Pitzer College.

HARRY C. BOYTE is the founder and codirector of the Center for Democracy and Citizenship and a senior fellow at the Humphrey Institute. His recent works include *Everyday Politics* (University of Pennsylvania Press, 2004) and *The Citizen Solution*, forthcoming from the Minnesota Historical Society and Kettering Foundation Press. He was national coordinator of the national New Citizenship coalition and is now helping to organize the Civic Agency Initiative with the American Association of State Colleges and Universities.

DAVID W. BROWN is coeditor of the *Higher Education Exchange*. He taught at Yale's School of Management, New School's Milano Graduate School, authored *When Strangers Cooperate* (Free Press, 1995) and *Organization Smarts* (Amacon, 2002), and coedited *Agent of Democracy* (Kettering Foundation Press, 2008). He has also practiced law and served as a state commissioner, deputy mayor, public authority board member, and college president.

DAVID D. COOPER is Professor of Writing, Rhetoric, and American Cultures at Michigan State University and University Outreach and Engagement Senior Fellow. He is founder and current director of MSU's Public Humanities Collaborative (www.phc.msu.edu). The author of several books, Cooper is photo essay editor of the literary nonfiction journal *Fourth Genre* and an active photo essayist, with a strong interest in documentary photography as an agent of social change.

ALLISON N. CRAWFORD is currently a student at the University of Georgia School of Law. She is a graduate of Wake Forest University where she studied political science and English.

SEAN CREIGHTON is the Executive Director of the Southwestern Ohio Council for Higher Education, a regional consortium of colleges and universities dedicated to advancing higher education through collaboration. He has published research on civic engagement in the *Higher Education Exchange*, *Journal of Civic Commitment*, and *Metropolitan Universities Journal* and he has a chapter forthcoming in *Service-Learning in Higher Education: Paradigms and Challenges*. Creighton is an elected board member for the Yellow Springs School District, and also a clinical assistant professor at Wright State University. In 2006, he earned his PhD in Leadership and Change from Antioch University.

JONI DOHERTY is director of the New England Center for Civic Life and teaches in the American Studies Program at Franklin Pierce University. She is editor of the College Issues Forums, a series of discussion guides developed in collaboration with students and faculty at Franklin Pierce, and she directs the Diversity & Community Project, an initiative developed to foster awareness of and respect for diversity.

WILLIAM J. DOHERTY is a professor in the Department of Family Social Science and director of the Citizen Professional Center at the University of Minnesota. He leads the Citizen Health Care and Families and Democracy Project, which fosters civic action by families and democratic public work by professionals. He and his colleagues currently have 13 grassroots organizing projects among parents and other citizens on issues ranging from the cultural discontents of middle-class families (overscheduling, out-of-control birthday parties) to challenges of urban single fathers, and from diabetes among American Indians to the school/family disconnect in African immigrant communities.

ALBERT W. DZUR is Associate Professor of Political Science and a Senior Research Fellow at the Social Philosophy & Policy Center at Bowling Green State University. His work on civic engagement focuses on the value of lay participation in professional and expert domains, such as through citizen boards in criminal justice, public forums in journalism, and ethics committees in medicine. His book *Democratic Professionalism: Citizen Participation and the Reconstruction of Professional Ethics, Identity, and Practice* was published in spring 2008 by Penn State University Press. His current research examines the development of a more democratic professional identity within the university.

KATY J. HARRIGER is a professor of political science at Wake Forest University where she teaches courses on American politics, courts, democracy, and citizenship. Harriger is the editor of *Separation of Powers: Commentaries and Documents* (Congressional Quarterly Press, 2003) and the author of *The Special Prosecutor in American Politics*, 2nd ed. revised (University Press of Kansas, 2000) and *Independent Justice: The Federal Special Prosecutor in American Politics* (University Press of Kansas, 1992), as well as a number of articles in journals and law reviews. She can be reached by e-mail at harriger@wfu.edu.

MATTHEW HARTLEY is a faculty member at the University of Pennsylvania's Graduate School of Education. His research and writing focus on academic governance and organizational change at colleges and universities. He is especially interested in exploring how academic communities define their educational missions. His current research examines the democratic purposes of American higher education. Hartley earned his EdM and EdD from Harvard University's Graduate School of Education.

ELIZABETH HOLLANDER is currently Senior Fellow at the Tisch College of Citizenship and Public Service. From 1997 to 2006, she served as Executive Director of Campus Compact. Prior to her tenure at Campus Compact, she was founding director of an urban center at DePaul University and had a career in urban development that included six years as the Commissioner of Planning for the city of Chicago.

NAN KARI has pursued work for democratic renewal in a variety of contexts since the late 1980s. She was a faculty member at the College of St. Catherine for 20 years and led efforts to revitalize the public culture at the college. She has published many articles and a book on public work and civic renewal. She is a cofounder of the Jane Addams School for Democracy.

ABBY KIESA is Youth Coordinator and Researcher at CIRCLE (www. civicyouth.org), a national research center on young people's civic education and engagement. At CIRCLE she serves as liaison to practitioner organizations across the country. She communicates research findings and tracks recommendations from young people, youth-serving organizations, and educators for future research. Kiesa is currently working on a large project focused on young people who do not have college experience. Prior to CIRCLE, she organized students around the country as part of a national campaign of Campus Compact to increase student involvement in public life and coedited *Raise Your Voice: A Student Guide to Making Positive Social Change.*

DAVID MATHEWS, president of the Kettering Foundation, was secretary of Health, Education, and Welfare in the Ford administration and, before that, president of The University of Alabama. He has written extensively on education, political theory, Southern history, public policy, and international problem solving. He has written several books, including *Why Public Schools? Whose Public Schools?* (NewSouth Books, 2003); *For Communities to Work* (Kettering Foundation, 2002); and a revised second edition of *Politics for People* (University of Illinois Press, 1999). His newest book, *Reclaiming Public Education by Reclaiming Our Democracy* (Kettering Foundation Press, 2006) focuses on the relationship between the public and public education.

JILL J. MCMILLAN is professor emerita at Wake Forest University. Having been a member of the Deliberative Democracy Workshop sponsored by the Kettering Foundation since 2000, McMillan continues to write and speak on the pedagogy of deliberative democracy in higher education. Her other recent publications have considered matters of organizational rhetoric and the communicative dimensions of corporate social responsibility.

KERRYANN O'MEARA is Associate Professor of Higher Education at the University of Maryland. Her research explores the structures, cultures, and systems in colleges and universities that support and sometimes impede faculty careers and the ability of faculty to develop as well-rounded professionals, and thereby contribute to the development of others. She serves as the associate editor of the *Journal of Higher Education Outreach and*

Engagement. She is the author of the book *Scholarship Unbound: Assessing Service as Scholarship for Promotion and Tenure*, published by Routledge-Falmer, and coauthor of the monograph *Faculty Careers and Work-Lives: A Professional Growth Perspective*, coming out with ASHE.

DAVID PELLETIER is a biological anthropologist with an MA/PhD from The Pennsylvania State University in 1979/1984. He joined the Division of Nutritional Sciences at Cornell University as a postdoctoral associate in 1984, where he conducted nutrition research and policy/program work in developing countries. In 1994, he began a tenure-track faculty position at Cornell. His primary interests relate to developing, applying, and evaluating improved methods for policy analysis and development at community and national levels, with a special focus on the integration of scientific/technical information and social/normative considerations through methods for direct public involvement. He can be reached by e-mail at dlp5@cornell.edu.

SCOTT J. PETERS is an associate professor in the Department of Education at Cornell University. His research program combines the study of the history of American higher education's public purposes and work with a narrative approach to the study of the civic practices and experiences of contemporary academic professionals and community educators. He can be reached by e-mail at sp236@cornell.edu.

JAY ROSEN is on the faculty of the Arthur L. Carter Journalism Institute at New York University. Rosen is the author of PressThink, a weblog about journalism and its ordeals (www.pressthink.org). In 1999, Yale University Press published his book, *What Are Journalists For?*, which is about the rise of the civic journalism movement.

MARGUERITE S. SHAFFER graduated from the University of Pennsylvania and received her PhD in the History of American Civilization from Harvard University. She is the Director of American Studies and Associate Professor of American Studies and history at Miami University in Oxford, Ohio. She is the author of *See America First: Tourism and National Identity, 1880-1940* (Smithsonian Institution Press, 2001) and editor of *Public Culture: Diversity, Democracy, and Community in the United States* (University of Pennsylvania Press, 2008). Her current work focuses on issues of public culture and popular environmentalism in the United States.

NAN SKELTON codirects the Center for Democracy and Citizenship at the Humphrey Institute of Public Affairs. She has been engaged in many civic projects. Throughout the 1980s, she served as the Assistant Commissioner for Education for the state of Minnesota and continues to lead educational reform efforts. She is a cofounder of the Jane Addams School for Democracy.

ADAM WEINBERG is the Provost and Executive Vice President at World Learning/SIT. Weinberg joined World Learning in December 2005 from Colgate University, where he held a number of faculty positions since 1994, including Vice President and Dean of the College from 2002 to 2005. He has written extensively on the ways universities can be resources for addressing local and national needs. Weinberg was also the architect of Colgate's Residential Education program, which has attracted significant national attention for its innovative approach to civic education. At World Learning, he oversees academic programs in over 50 countries.